Sixty-five Sunsets

A CANADIAN WEST COAST JOURNEY

A summer spent exploring the coastline of British Columbia by kayak to experience the people and the wilderness of the Pacific Northwest

RICK DAVIES AND JAQUIE BUNSE

Note for Librarians: A cataloguing record for this book is available from Library and Archives Canada at www.collectionscanada.ca/amicus/index-e.html
ISBN 1-4120-8091-6

Printed in Victoria, BC, Canada. Printed on paper with minimum 30% recycled fibre. Trafford's print shop runs on "green energy" from solar, wind and other environmentally-friendly power sources.

Cover Photo by Jaquie Bunse
Cover Design by Meticulous Graphics and Design Inc.

Offices in Canada, USA, Ireland and UK
This book was published *on-demand* in cooperation with Trafford Publishing. On-demand publishing is a unique process and service of making a book available for retail sale to the public taking advantage of on-demand manufacturing and Internet marketing. On-demand publishing includes promotions, retail sales, manufacturing, order fulfilment, accounting and collecting royalties on behalf of the author.

Book sales for North America and international:
Trafford Publishing, 6E–2333 Government St.,
Victoria, BC V8T 4P4 CANADA
phone 250 383 6864 (toll-free 1 888 232 4444)
fax 250 383 6804; email to orders@trafford.com
Book sales in Europe:
Trafford Publishing (UK) Limited, 9 Park End Street, 2nd Floor
Oxford, UK OX1 1HH UNITED KINGDOM
phone 44 (0)1865 722 113 (local rate 0845 230 9601)
facsimile 44 (0)1865 722 868; info.uk@trafford.com
Order online at:
trafford.com/05-3089

10 9 8 7 6 5 4 3 2

This book is dedicated to
Sally, Kristin, Mark, Scott, Sam and Kaitlyn

May they follow their own paths
Not where convention dictates
But where their passions lie

Contents

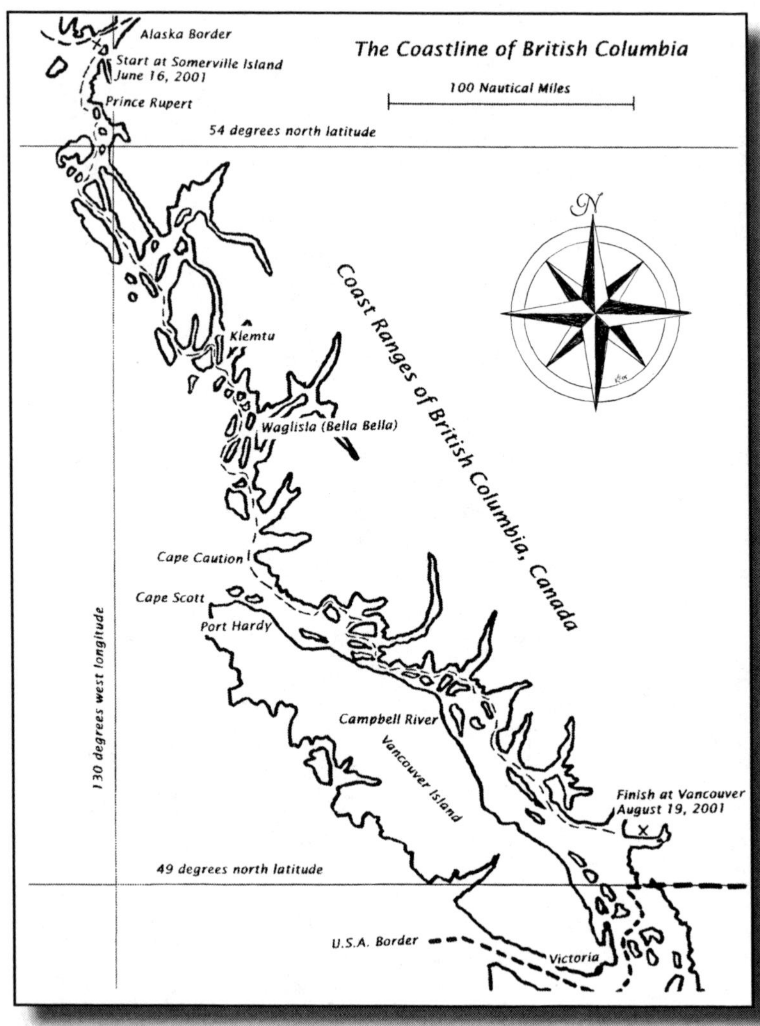

The Coastline of British Columbia
100 Nautical Miles
Alaska Border
Start at Somerville Island
June 16, 2001
Prince Rupert
54 degrees north latitude
N
Coast Ranges of British Columbia, Canada
Klemtu
Waglisla (Bella Bella)
Cape Caution
Cape Scott
Port Hardy
Campbell River
Vancouver Island
130 degrees west longitude
Finish at Vancouver
August 19, 2001
49 degrees north latitude
U.S.A. Border
Victoria

Prologue

Putting The Passion Into Action

The germination process started around Christmas of 2000. Jaquie and I were enjoying our usual winter of backcountry ski touring, snow camping and the occasional day on the downhill slopes of our local mountains. The thought of cruising summer waters and landing on remote sunny beaches looked distinctly attractive from the viewpoint of a dark Vancouver winter day. We casually discussed the prospect of doing a long trip together and I found myself buying the odd chart or two. We pored over them in the evenings and slowly realized what was involved. As weeks passed, I had accumulated twenty-five charts having spent $500. Okay, I'm a chart junkie and I admit it.

On seeing this huge stack of charts on the living room floor, we pondered upon how we would carry all of them in our kayaks. Should we pack them whole or cut them down to save weight and bulk? From a navigator's standpoint, deliberately cutting up a chart is sacrilege and found I couldn't do it. It felt to me like tearing a well-loved book to pieces.

There was a deeper personal reason to have these charts to share our experience. Years from now we will relive the journey, reminiscing over our journals and photos. My charts must have been there with us! I wonder if other travellers think of maps and charts in this way?

My maps and charts of worldwide adventures have been collected since 1957. Many are torn, muddy, water marked, bearing food and bloodstains. Most have marks and comments, showing routes, bearings, obstacles, traverse times, shortcuts and hazards. The common denominator among them is having shared my experience. Do maps have souls? Frivolous thought, but I know that on occasions of personal "extremis", a map has been more valuable to me than food, and I have the utmost respect for them!

We discussed laminating the charts to waterproof them but concluded the bulk of fifty was unmanageable. In the end we took them intact, packed into a thirty litre dry bag, creating a package eighteen inches square by six inches deep. They occupied a major part of the rear compartment in my kayak in a Mountain Equipment Co-op dry bag capable of keeping them dry throughout the whole trip. It was beneficial to have the complete charts as we diverged from our planned track to take advantage of the good weather on the outside, or to follow an enticing whim during the journey. We avoid navigating blind, so using a very small-scale chart with little detail makes life more difficult and potentially dangerous indeed.

Evening after winter evening at home found me kneeling at the coffee table, thoroughly plotting a track, mile by mile down the coast to ensure that we could complete the journey by the beginning of September. We each had business commitments after this date and didn't want to feel pressured to rush day after day. We wanted to *live* along the BC coast — to experience the people, wildlife and most of all ourselves. To do this satisfactorily we would eliminate the pressure of a tight schedule.

I calculated 532 nautical miles total distance then added a "fudge factor" of 15% extra for delays, storms and route diversions. This gave us an overall daily average of eight nautical miles a day. In fact, we travelled a total of 602 nautical miles, a 20% increase over our original plan, with an average of ten miles per day. When calculated just on paddling days, it worked out to twelve miles per day with nine days off for rest or storms.

Previous kayak trips had stretched as long a month, but this endeavour was the equivalent of three years of recreational kayaking. Wear and tear on equipment accelerates quickly with heavy daily use, and our concerns were compounded by the fact that there would be little opportunity to replace much of it. We needed to carry nylon fabric to repair clothing and stuff bags, a sailmaker's palm for sewing heavy material, waxed thread, epoxy, fibreglass repair compound, tools and, of course, duct tape. We used every item during the trip. Many evenings on the beach were spent sewing, gluing and reforming items of equipment showing signs of strain. Nature's assault on synthetics was illustrated by the condition of my camera case when we reached Vancouver. My waterproof Canon Sureshot rode on my upper deck, always secured with the flap side uppermost. When we beached on the last day, the underside was still bright red, whereas the exposed side was bleached almost white by ultraviolet and salt spray.

The number of spare items we would normally take on a three or four day trip increased considerably, together with the corresponding increase in bulk and weight. For example we took 48 AA dry cells, 20 films, 5 candles for the lantern and so on. We deliberated over taking "luxury items," finally deciding that some extra weight was worth carrying. Our philosophy is comfortable slow travel, rather than breaking speed records. Jaquie brought a small backgammon game for long days stormed inside the tent, we started with two novels each and a tiny transistor radio. The arsenal of pyrotechnics included a parachute flare, although I really didn't know who would be out there to see it. If in trouble, we knew it would be up to us to solve the problem or perish trying.

Our energies must be directed on self-help, so we carried only a VHF marine radio and flares. Although satellite phone or EPIRB (emergency position indicator radio beacon) technology is available, we opted for simpler solutions. This decision could have been disastrous but Fortune smiled on us. Technology is limited anyway. The VHF was unable to pick up a weather forecast for two days in Principe Channel and I couldn't have sent a distress signal out if I had needed to. There may be no ship traffic for several days in some areas, so visual distress signals may not always be effective.

Navigation instruments we carried included a magnetic compass with two spares as backup, and a set of "Shipmaster" tide and current tables. Perhaps a GPS (global positioning system) receiver would have been useful if we had travelled in fog offshore, but our strategy was to wait for fog to clear before crossing a shipping lane. We tended to use the shoreline as a "handrail" provided there were not too many offshore boomers (reefs with breaking seas) forcing us out to sea.

"Shipmaster" tide and current tables has an excellent range of current and tide secondaries which are invaluable in complicated tidal areas such as Johnstone Strait, where the meeting of the tides around Vancouver Island create some surprising anomalies.

Stories circulate about kayakers doing this same trip using only a BC road map! How they succeeded in traversing the major tidal rapids amazed us. The gauntlet in the nip between Vancouver Island and mainland forced us to take one of three routes through very serious tidal rapids. There is no other way - not the best place to have a road map with a scale of fifteen miles to the inch.

To plan and organize our food, we used a "Pantry" system rather than a "Menu" system. Our meals were created on the spot from bulk staples rather than having all the meals preweighed and packaged. The pantry system has the advantage of flexibility and choice as well as easier packing. The menu system has the advantage of simplicity and speed of meal preparation. Our delicious range of culinary creations included fresh soup and chowder, pizza, baked pasta, bread, brownies, cornbread, cheesecake, muffins, cookies, upside-down cake, chicken pot pie, iced cake and focaccia bread.

Our initial load of food weighed 200 pounds for the first unsupported month. Thereafter we relied on purchasing replacement goods along the way, rather than pre-arranging food drops. This allowed us flexibility in our course, and in the worst-case scenario we could partially live off the sea and the shore. We wanted the freedom to change the route or by-pass certain stops without fear of running short of staples. We consequently made the decision to by-pass Port Hardy in favour of exploring the Northern Broughton Archipelago. A pre-arranged food drop at Port Hardy would have restricted our flexibility considerably. We found Native band stores were excellent sources of all the things we needed. We stocked up in Kitkatla, Klemtu & Bella Bella. Marina shops, on the other hand, were less useful to us as they often lack staples such as oatmeal, rice or yeast. Cigarettes, camera film and chocolate bars are great if you're running a powerboat loaded with months of food, but our capacity was limited. Our needs were more basic and required olive oil, flour or white gas.

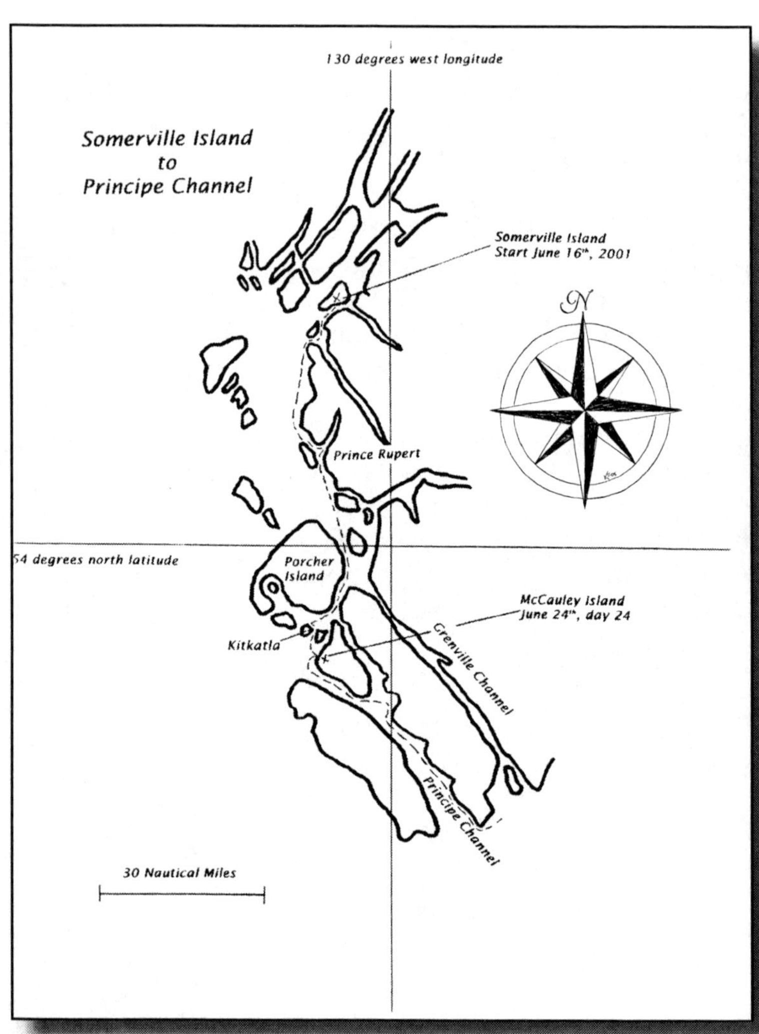
130 degrees west longitude
Somerville Island
to
Principe Channel
Somerville Island
Start June 16th, 2001
N
Prince Rupert
54 degrees north latitude
Porcher
Island
McCauley Island
June 24th, day 24
Kitkatla
Grenville Channel
Principe Channel
30 Nautical Miles

Well, We're Here:

The North Coast

When you undertake a long journey, it is extremely unwise to start off looking forward to the end. If you do, you are effectively negating the enjoyment of every day, every hour, every minute. You are bridging your psyche over too many precious experiences and letting them go to waste. Our trip was not sixty-five days so much as sixty-five day trips, each one linked to the other. The watchword for an extended journey is... **Carpe diem.**

At nine o'clock in the morning on June 16, 2001, our water transporters, Don and Walter, backed a pick-up truck into the driveway of the B & B in Prince Rupert. We packed all of our gear bags into the truck box, then tied the kayaks on top of the load. In town we picked up a few last minute items and extra fuel for the boat before our arrival at the marina launch ramp.

We lashed our kayaks to the fishing boat, one along each side of the wheelhouse. We packed the rest of the gear into every available space, crowding the four of us into the wheelhouse. Our excitement building, we cast off at eleven-thirty.

As we made our way north from Prince Rupert to our drop off point in the Portland Canal, we listened closely to Don. Skimming up the coast, weaving deftly through the reefs, he told us what we might expect to encounter when we retraced today's speedy journey. We estimated it would take us four kayaking days to get back down to Prince Rupert. We drew every scrap of information we could from him.

Don's local knowledge proved very valuable in the days to follow, although we were to discover many powerboat operators along the way who didn't really understand areas of vital importance to kayakers. When a kayaker asks a powerboat skipper for details such as, "What are the currents like on the ebb at the mouth of Work Channel?" the captain may reply, "Yes, be careful. The wind really rips around that corner on a westerly." Powerboat skippers are careful about the wind, but might not be concerned with currents when they have so much horsepower at their disposal. They nudge the throttle up a notch and power out of trouble. But this isn't the case for those of us who have only 'armstrong' power. With a maximum of four knots at a short burst, a current above two knots must be carefully calculated, as it will have a big impact on progress.

After a ninety-minute cruise, Don and Walter dropped us off on our white sandy beach on an ebbing tide. In the time it took us to unload our two kayaks and our mountain of gear, it went out fast. The 22-foot tide range around the solstice on the North Coast provided us with endless challenges. The first of these was that we had to rock, twist and push Don and Walter's fishing boat off the sand and into deep enough water to allow it to move off. The two men looked much relieved. They likely didn't relish spending another twelve hours on the beach until the next high tide at eleven o'clock that night, especially where they would have had to watch us paddle blithely off.

"Well, we're here, Jaquie! This is the start." We stood on the beach contemplating the task of stuffing 300 pounds of clothing, food and hardware into these two frail boats. Were we out of our minds?

With the fishing vessel gone, the silence of the beautiful white sandy beach set in. We let its power overtake us as we stood on Somerville Island, just south of the Alaska border. After the noise of the city, ferries, highways and multitudes of voices, the roar of the engine in the fishing boat, there was suddenly… nothing. The sea sat glassy calm before us. No wind disturbed it, and the fishing boat disappeared into the distance on its way back to Prince Rupert. This was indeed a significant moment – the start of our journey.

It took an hour to pack up and launch into Steamer Passage. I paddle a Nimbus "Seafarer" with 450-litre capacity, one of the highest capacity single person kayak available. Jaquie uses an older version of the Nimbus "Solander" with a slightly smaller volume, but between us we were able to pack our first month's food and equipment without too much trouble. Although we had done a dry run at home, there were still those few extra items picked up along the way or not taken into account. Each kayak had a thirty-litre drybag lashed onto the rear deck. These contained extra food or other items we needed close at hand or which didn't fit inside the hull. We packed very carefully to ensure our safety gear was readily available and unencumbered by deck baggage. Spare paddles must never be trapped under a deck bag, tow lines must be free to deploy without fouling. Paddle float self-rescue devices must pull free without releasing anything that could tangle in a capsize situation. The safest approach is to assume that anything not securely lashed down will be lost. If caught in a sudden squall there is no time to start tying everything down.

Neither of us came anywhere near capsizing on this trip – partly due to our very wide safety margins, but also because the boats were heavily laden and therefore extremely stable. So stable, in fact, that my normally cautious method of entry became relaxed. I found I could sit on the rear deck, push off from shore and then slip into the cockpit at my leisure. I wouldn't try this with a lightly loaded, less stable kayak, as I would be over in the blink of an eye. Climbing out onto a dock is equally easy with fully loaded boats. We simply grabbed the dock, stood up on the seat, and stepped out.

Eager to begin, we hadn't noticed the change in conditions as we packed. We moved off under a grey sky on a black sea with growing whitecaps. *Our first mile!* After a slog down Steamer Passage, we eased into the relative shelter of Emma Passage, then on to Paradise Passage and Work Channel. Even though we could have reached Work Channel by vehicle via logging roads from Prince Rupert, it would have added an extra fifty miles of paddling to the trip. We mused that this approach might still be a viable option for other trips, and might reduce the cost we'd incurred hiring Don and Walter.

Our first camp was on Maskelyne Island, in a less-than-picturesque gully choked with damp bush. We experienced the first of many rough landings and tough haul-outs. We were weary. Baked beans, smoked salmon, and coffee were all we attempted, and the combination made adequate fare for our supper.

Opening half an eye on June 17, I heard light rain falling on the tent. *Hey, this is the North Coast!* I crawled out of the tent and lit the fire, and we devoted a long, lazy breakfast to waiting for the tide to come in. At eleven o'clock we launched into the narrow channel on the high tide to avoid lowering the boats down the steep rocks, then set off towards the village of Lax Kw'alaams, formerly Port Simpson.

Threading our way down the channel, Jaquie seemed preoccupied, concentrating intensely on something and utterly unwilling to join in any conversation. My comments of "Beautiful coastline" or, "Look at that salmon jump" were met with a studied frown and a shake of her head. Puzzled, I paddled on for another half an hour, covering a nautical mile. Suddenly she triumphantly announced, "A thousand paddle strokes per mile!"

All became abundantly clear. Based on her count, we would each execute over half a million paddle strokes on our way to Vancouver. What a staggering thought –and especially at the beginning of a trip!

Our snack break at Picnic Point on Birnie Island seemed idyllic as the sun came out to warm our bodies. A two-mile crossing took us close to the forested setting of Lax Kw'alaams.

Jaquie:

The village first appeared below a clear cut. The red roof of the church dominated the surrounding dwellings. Along the rocky shoreline and on rooftops sat many bald eagles, juvenile and adult, marking our progress like watchmen as we paddled past. I was torn between the desire to stop and visit the village, learn about its people and history – and the concern of intruding upon the privacy and peacefulness we felt as we passed. Determination to learn about our environment set in, although I knew it would wait until the opportunity arose later in the trip.

When at home again, I emailed Wayne Drury, the Administrator of the Lax Kw'alaams Band and asked him for information about the history of the band and the village. He wrote:

> Port Simpson was established in 1834 at Lax Kw'alaams, a traditional Tsimshian camping location by the Hudson's Bay Company. From 1831-1834, Port Simpson was located on the Nass River. The name Lax Kw'alaams means 'roses', a reference to the wild roses that used to grow on the island just off the shore from the Hudson Bay Fort and main part of the community. In the same year, one of the Tsimshian Tribes, the Gispaxlo'ots, relocated from the Skeena River to Port Simpson, under Chief Ligeex.
>
> Port Simpson emerged as a major Tsimshian village location. There were several epidemics of diseases at Port

Simpson – measles in 1848, smallpox in 1862 and 1898, and measles on the upper Skeena River in 1877-1878.

The Lax Kw'alaams Band is the second largest in British Columbia, and the community is the centre and the home for nine of the 14 tribes that make up the total Tsimshian First Nation. The remaining five tribes are located in Hartley Bay, Kitkatla, Kitselas, Kitsumkalum and Kitasoo.

Port Simpson is now a community of 1300, of a total 2900 members of the Lax Kw'alaams Band. This vibrant community is building its economy on the back of the resources that are part of its traditional territory and part of the tribes through assertion of aboriginal rights and title.

Five years ago the community was mired in debt, and on the brink of bankruptcy, but the community leaders have engineered an almost unheard of turnaround. The community faced 85% unemployment, 50% of the community was on welfare, a disturbing number of suicides occurred every year, the band staggered under a $5million annual debt, and the people were saddled with an educational system that has possibly delivered the greatest failure rates in British Columbia.

Through the work of the Band Council, the band has secured more than $5.5 million in surpluses in the past three years and developed new health and mental health programmes that have almost eliminated suicides (there has not been one for two years). An educational turnaround shows attendance at school has increased from less than 50% to more than 90%. Welfare rolls have dropped to less than 3% of the population, unemployment has dropped to less than 10%, and the community has the financial resources to add an $8.5 million community centre, including aquatic centre and 150-foot water slide for the community.

This community is moving forward in its objective to satisfy social, economic, safety, health, and cultural goals that reflect the values that are most important to the band and community membership. The Band Council has assisted the nine Tribes of Lax Kw'alaams to assert aboriginal rights and title to the land and resources within their traditional territory that will further enable economic and social development to benefit the band membership.

Wayne Drury, Administrator
Lax Kw'alaams Band

Running south past Lax Kw'alaams, we found the ebb pushing north against us through Cunningham Passage. We worked the back eddies. Using one of the tricks of kayak travel, we took advantage of places where the main current splits in two, sending water in the opposite direction around a bay. We cruised through the bays then thrashed around the headlands in quick bursts, taking advantage of every little eddy, no matter how close to shore, working quite easily against the main current. We repeated this technique so often that it became automatic. Paddle hard around the point, relax and recover in the eddy, and repeat over and over and over.

We passed three abandoned fish boats listing at crazy angles, some visibly holed, high and dry at Hook Point Bay – a graveyard silent and brooding. This may be a symptom of declining fishing opportunities on the coast – someone's livelihood or dream lying rotting on the rocks. It seemed sad, but served as an illustration of the changing economies of the West Coast. Carving out a living is tough on the coast, physically and financially. Along our trip we listened to many stories of dreams, some of which failed to reach fruition, others which demonstrated the strength and determination of the people who stayed and succeeded. And we understood the great temptation for youth to move to the city.

At the exit from Cunningham Passage we pulled up on the most easterly of the Flat Top Islands. This was one of the most beautiful campsites we'd seen, largely because of the perfect weather provided by a growing high-pressure ridge – a good omen for the voyage ahead. We sunbathed until we were hungry then built a fire to cook our supper. A glass of wine complemented the perfect location as we looked out to the abrupt square shape of Burnt Cliff Island, a mile to the south. Our pebbled spit of land gradually faded in the dusk as the huge orange sun sank into a burning sea to the west and the Milky Way slowly appeared in the deep dark of the night sky.

A Dall's porpoise and a river otter each in turn gave us a breakfast show in glassy calm water. While we watched them, we toasted bagels, smeared them with honey, and munched on dried prunes that we washed down with hot coffee.

Three hours elapsed from the time we got up to the time we had our kayaks on the water. *Ah well, nowhere in particular to get to and all day to do it.* We believe our packing time will shorten with practice. Our heavy boats slid into the calm sea, past the east coast of Burnt Cliff Island, and skimmed across the shallow sand flats. After two miles across Big Bay in flat calm, we took our first snack break at Trenham Point Beach.

This part of the coast is littered with large underwater boulders, which are difficult to avoid, especially if you are paddling into the sun. If you choose to do this journey from north to south, the sun is in your eyes all the way, a definite drawback. With the sun reflecting on the water, colours are not so vivid, and you cannot see obstacles just under the surface, increasing your chances of grounding on a reef. With a light boat it's not normally a great hazard, but on an extended trip and at a speed of three knots with 400 pounds of boat, striking a rock can do considerable damage to a kayak.

The next five miles were spent weaving our way through rock gardens and sand flats past Tree Bluff, Slippery Rock, Swamp Island, and finally to Ryan Point – places that Don had noted for us during our journey up the coast. We debated over going out to Tugwell Island to camp or continuing into Duncan Bay. The bay won out. The forecast called for 35-knot winds from the south. We opted to visit Prince Rupert to pick up a few small items we thought would make life easier. Paddling west to Tugwell, we would have by-passed Prince Rupert altogether.

Jaquie:

My habit is to set a goal or two for major expeditions. On this trip, my first hope is to make it all the way to Vancouver under my own steam.

Today, the enormity of the coast we will travel has just dawned upon me. However did I get myself here? Am I mad? Can I really pull my own weight, be an equal member of our tiny team of two? The voices of my friends, my children, and colleagues are in my head – they truly believe that I can do it, so I guess somehow I just will.

With all these hours on the water to think, my mind must have a puzzle to solve. I will allow myself lots of daydreaming about work for the fall and winter. When I return, will I allow myself the luxury of flexible hours, lots of variety and stimulation? Beneath my stolid Protestant work ethic and my need for achievement is a quiet rumble of "But I'm 54. I'm getting tired of working." Where did this voice come from? Will I create a job that offers enough to live on and meet my needs in other ways?

That night we wound our way into the one and only landing in Duncan Bay, a beautiful shell beach tucked away amidst a host of jagged black reefs. The southern sky looked ominous with a bank of blue-grey nimbus stretching from horizon to horizon. A solid low-pressure system with a warm front was coming in off the Pacific, but we were too tired to worry about the next day. We walked like ninety-year-olds, stiff with lifting and carrying our gear, still unaccustomed to the long hours of paddling over the first two days of the journey.

This had been only the third day of the trip and I'd developed tendonitis in my left elbow, a condition which dogged me for the next sixty-three days. Although never severe enough to stop me from paddling, it prevented me from straightening my arm throughout the entire trip. In the past, this condition had been relieved by tricks like rotating my paddles to a non-feathered position (both blades flat) or shifting the paddle to shorten the torque on my injured side. But this time, none of these tricks worked. I knew the common-sense remedy was to stop paddling for a few months. But since this was impossible, I used the 'grin-and-bear-it' technique. Months after the trip ended, the tenderness would linger.

Duncan Bay shaped up as a snug camp, our comfort augmented by fresh potatoes, cabbage, and vegetable stew for supper. We were delighted at the way cabbage stays fresh for weeks, and is good either cooked or raw in salads. It became an important item to replenish along with onions, garlic, carrots, and fresh fruit whenever it was available.

Although we'd battened down tight in our high tech mountain tent for the storm we expected that night, it didn't materialize. Still, a threatening sky glowered as we packed our gear, launched through the black, jagged reefs and moved off towards Prince Rupert. After crossing the bay, we struggled through huge rafts of kelp, fought the flood current, and pushed into an increasing southerly wind as we approached Observation Point. Once around it we had the luxury of being carried along Venn Passage by the current entering Prince Rupert Harbour. After a brief respite, we battled our way across the last mile of open water to the city waterfront, pushing tired muscles and tendons nearly to their limits. The undulating topography of the seabed created some challenging peculiarities in the waves, causing chop and upwelling areas that took us off balance, and sometimes it seemed we made no headway at all.

Much relieved to arrive in the lee of the Prince Rupert seawall, we were determined that we were going to stay the night in Prince Rupert to recuperate. Rain and wind lashed our starboard bows as we hauled across to the shelter of the main wharf area. A short burst along the shore landed us in Cow Bay at the float owned by *Ecotreks*, a local kayak outfitter.

Rain bucketed down as it only can in Prince Rupert, and we pondered our next move. First the Yellow Pages at the phone booth on the wharf –resulting in a room at the Rainforest Bed & Breakfast. Don and Cindy made us very welcome, meeting us at the waterfront, giving us directions to their home, and transporting our wet gear to the B & B for us. We locked our boats to the float, then set out to explore.

The wind howled out of the southerly quarter, storming us in for the next two days. But it has been said that everything happens for a good reason. Our forced stay turned out to be both fruitful and interesting.

Gear improvement is always in the back of my mind, and I plotted to reduce strain on our bodies and boats. Our system for hoisting food clear of wildlife is a hook and pulley that fits over the end of a paddle blade. We stretch up at arm's length plus the height of a paddle, lodging the hook over a sturdy branch. Then we haul the food up with a rope through the pulley, tying it off to secure it. This system is superior to throwing a rock inside a bag over the branch, a method that often ends up knocking the thrower on the head, tangling the line or failing to get the line over the branch at all.

Two hundred pounds of food appeared to require a second, lighter-weight aluminum food-hauling hook. To make food caches safer, lighter and easier to hoist into trees, I designed a simple device and had it made at a local metal fabricating shop.

An obliging tradesman cheerfully promised it would be ready the next day. True to his word, he produced the finished article the next morning, a beautiful high-tensile aluminum hook with an eye, made exactly to our specifications, and an improvement over our first model.

At first we felt restless and discontent at the prospect of waiting for two days in Prince Rupert, especially where we were only four days into a sixty-five day trip. But predicaments can turn into opportunities, and we were about to learn a bit about fish farming. David Suzuki was in town, and we attended a presentation by the Suzuki Foundation at a local hotel. Hearing points of view from the different factions and interest groups at the meeting gave us background information that we debated while we passed the farms along the coast. The presentations by First Nations, fishers, and other citizens were passionate as they stated their case for or against the farms. We walked back to the B & B in a sober mood, with a much deeper understanding of the people and the challenges of the North Coast.

Our forced stay in town was an opportunity to repair equipment and rest and to pick up art supplies for painting 'spirit rocks' along the way. On the third day the weather moderated slightly, or perhaps we just convinced ourselves that the southerly had died down. We checked out of the B & B, hauled our gear down to the float, and put in after lunch. We battled our way out to the harbour limits in rain driven by a strong headwind. Two miles out of town, Jaquie remembered the three pounds of cheese and the dozen bagels she'd forgotten in the fridge at the B& B. But the thought of going back and doing battle with the wind again was too much, so we pushed on. We would have to get our protein and fats elsewhere.

Jaquie:

Solstice! The days will shorten for the rest of the trip. But how could I have forgotten to check the fridge before we left? Yesterday we trudged to several grocery stores, deliberating over the amount of cheese we could carry and the type of egg substitute we would most enjoy. The bagels were a grand assortment, fresh and warm when we took them out of the case. Worst of all is the cheese. I know how much Rick enjoys it, and it is such a good quick meal-maker. This is a reminder of my worries about pulling my weight on this trip, and I'm spending valuable energy on self-doubt. Time to let go of the mistake and move on.

Grinding slowly past Port Edward with its huge industrial facilities, we fought our way south for six hours into the wind and the current, without once getting out of the boats. Stopping long enough to dig out a granola bar lost us time and distance, even though we needed the energy.

The last two-mile crossing should have taken forty-five minutes, but we hit a two-knot northerly current coming straight off the Agnew Bank, forcing us to creep forward agonisingly slowly for an hour and a half to Kitson Island Marine Park. The buoy marking the edge of the sandbank seemed to stand still for ages, and as we drew closer, we noticed the extreme angle of lean as the current pushed it over in our direction. Kitson Island was a fuzzy objective somewhere ahead in the squalls.

When the island finally appeared through the rain, we gratefully headed around the east side to a secure camp on the south shore – glad to be out of town, out of the current, out of the wind, and on our own at last. The pasta and salmon supper was well earned that night, and before bed we lounged in a grassy hollow, safe from the storm.

Following the strenuous day, we allowed ourselves the luxury of a long, lazy morning on Kitson. After pancakes, oranges, and coffee we put in at noon, following the west coast of Smith Island down to Hazel Point. Now we were travelling along the ferry and cruise ship route running from Bella Bella to Prince Rupert. The flood was with us, a welcome treat after last night's struggle against the current. We made the top of Kennedy Island with some creative ferrying across currents and eddies. Two miles in thirty minutes without really exerting ourselves felt like a welcome type of paddling!

That night, upon reaching Lewis Island, close in to Porscher Island, we split up to search the shore for a suitable camp. At one stage I parked my boat and scrambled along the rocks, looking for a tent site. After walking round the point I met Jaquie in the next bay. What great opportunity to practise a "bow-carry" back to my boat. Bow-and stern-carries are standard techniques for rescuing a paddler if a boat should be lost or broken up. Jaquie carried me back to my boat on the bow of her kayak to practise a technique we might one day need in a hazardous situation.

We set up the tent on the only flat spot in sight with much concern for bears that might want to visit that night. An important rule of thumb is not to camp by a river mouth where bears are likely to be feeding on salmon. In fact, we were forced to break a few 'rules of thumb' on our journey, simply due to lack of choices. Reality modifies the best armchair planning.

Desperate searches for a camp at the end of a day sometimes yielded only a single flat space. The camping options on the North Coast present a variety of advantages and disadvantages. A camp in a rocky ravine or surge channel often lacks sufficient flat area for a comfortable tent and cooking site. Camps situated on game trails, or near creek outlets are areas visited frequently by bears and are potentially dangerous. If we sensed a strong chance we were intruding on some creature's territory, we blocked the path with brush and logs, brewed up plenty of tea, then 'marked' our territory on the brush and around our camp, giving the local wildlife fair warning of human guests on their turf. We were very careful to keep cooking and sleeping areas separate. We were generally diligent with cleanliness around camp and hung all our food and washing gear. Fortunately, we had no problems with wildlife throughout the trip.

An extremely low solstice tide the next day kept us on the beach until one in the afternoon. Our options were to carry everything through deep sucking mud for hundreds of yards to the water or to wait for the water to come to us. When we were finally able to put in, we worked the eddies to the south against the northerly flood, and arrived at Oona River, a historic small logging settlement on the southeast side of Porscher Island. It was there we met Terry, a Prince Rupert resident staying with friends for the weekend. He seemed curious about two lone kayakers so far from town. After a chat and a lot of questions, he and his friend contributed eggs and cheese to augment our diet. We were grateful for the generosity, but found it was typical of the kind folk we met all the way along our journey. We exchanged small talk, said our good-byes and set out to explore a little farther inland. After silently drifting along the tranquil inlet of Oona River, marveling at the near-perfect reflections in the still water, gazing at abandoned equipment from another age, we turned back to the sea. We were still months away from home, and remote by a full ten degrees of latitude.

Entering Ogden Channel, still heading clockwise around Porscher Island, we hit one of the worst downpours of the trip. Visibility was reduced to a few feet and even though there was no wind, rain churned the surface of the water into a frenzy. One of the advantages of sea kayaking over other methods of wilderness travel is that you can stay warm and snug, thanks not only to your waterproof parka and head covering, but to the spray skirt that seals tightly to your chest. There's a real sense of security in being dry and warm in what can sometimes be a hostile marine environment.

Later that afternoon we entered Skene Cove in a light rain and began our afternoon search for a camp. I set out around the cove, while Jaquie paddled over to greet the crew of a prawn boat that was anchored for the night. She asked if they knew of any camps in the area. Then I could see her laughing with them over gestures, waving arms, and apparently-heated arguments as they struggled with translations between English and Vietnamese. One of the crew pointed out a barely-visible notch in the shoreline across the cove, indicating a possible campsite. The skipper offered us prawns, Bacardi, fresh water, or anything else we needed. We declined the rum, Coca-Cola, and water, but accepted the prawns! That night, two dozen prawns sautéed in a honey garlic sauce and served with rice more than compensated for the wet, muddy environment and drizzle. We nicknamed this campsite "Slippery Camp" due to the many slips and slides we took in the greasy grey mud on the bank where we lit our dinner fire.

The deluge continued all night and we were glad we had taken a spacious three-person, four-season mountain tent with a vestibule. Many nights we camped in deep vegetation on forest floor that holds water like a sponge. We used our tarp *inside* the tent as a groundsheet and never had a wet night in the tent. Although we sometimes had to put up with a wet kitchen, the trade-off guaranteed a snug, dry sleep. In retrospect, a second tarp would have been a most valuable addition to our gear.

We waited out the morning in the tent until the rain stopped, and finally launched at two in the afternoon on Day Eight in clearing weather, leaving Skene Cove and Ogden Channel. Rounding Sparrowhawk Point, we wound through a maze of small emerald islands to Kitkatla Village. Numerous little floatplanes buzzed back and forth overhead, fishing boats passed us in every direction with the silent occupants tossing curious looks our way.

Kitkatla, population 500, is situated ideally on Dolphin Island just off the south end of Porscher Island. The name comes from a Coast Tsimshian word meaning “people of the salt” or “village by the sea”. The village is only a short distance from the open sea, but is sheltered from the full force of the Pacific. We beached to restock from the small store, photograph the picturesque church and longhouse, and indulge in junk food in the shape of chocolate bars and chips. We must have been an unusual sight, as small groups of children appeared around corners to look at us, smile shyly, and disappear with the occasional backward glance. A luxuriant tangle of fresh mint grew among the rocks, a reminder of the late North Coast spring. Jaquie picked a handful to add style and vitamins to our evening meal, offering thanks to anyone who might be listening.

Jaquie:

The Coast Tsimshian who wintered in Prince Rupert Harbour were well located to exploit a variety of resources and to participate in coastal and interior trade. In the early spring they migrated in kinship groups to the Nass River to trade and fish for eulachon. From there many people went to the outer islands to hunt sea mammals and gather shellfish. In summer, they moved to villages and campsites along the lower Skeena where they fished for salmon and gathered berries. In the late fall, their canoes loaded with dried salmon and trade goods, they returned to the winter villages.

Tsimshian society was divided into three classes: nobles, commoners, and slaves. Wealth was reflected in the clothing and personal adornments worn by the chiefs, their wives, and children. Nobles wore elaborate headdresses and helmets with crest images carved or painted on them. Their ceremonial clothing included woven Chilkat blankets, aprons and leggings. Following the introduction of European woollen cloth, a new type of clothing was made from dark blue trade blankets, decorated with red flannel crest designs and pearl buttons.

Satisfied by the sweet and salty snacks, and the chance to stretch our legs, we put in again and worked our way around Dolphin Island to Schooner Channel, one of the several passages to the open ocean. We timed our departure from Kitkatla to hit Schooner on the high slack tide to provide an easy paddle down and across Beaver Channel to McCauley Island. The exposed crossing turned out to be very easy and without incident. McCauley divides Petrel and Principe Channels, two of the three alternative routes we'd planned for the journey south to Bella Bella. We knew that we had to make a decision. We chose Principe, as it is about two miles wide, and offers enough open water to produce sandy beaches and a feeling of openness, compared to the gloom of the inner channels.

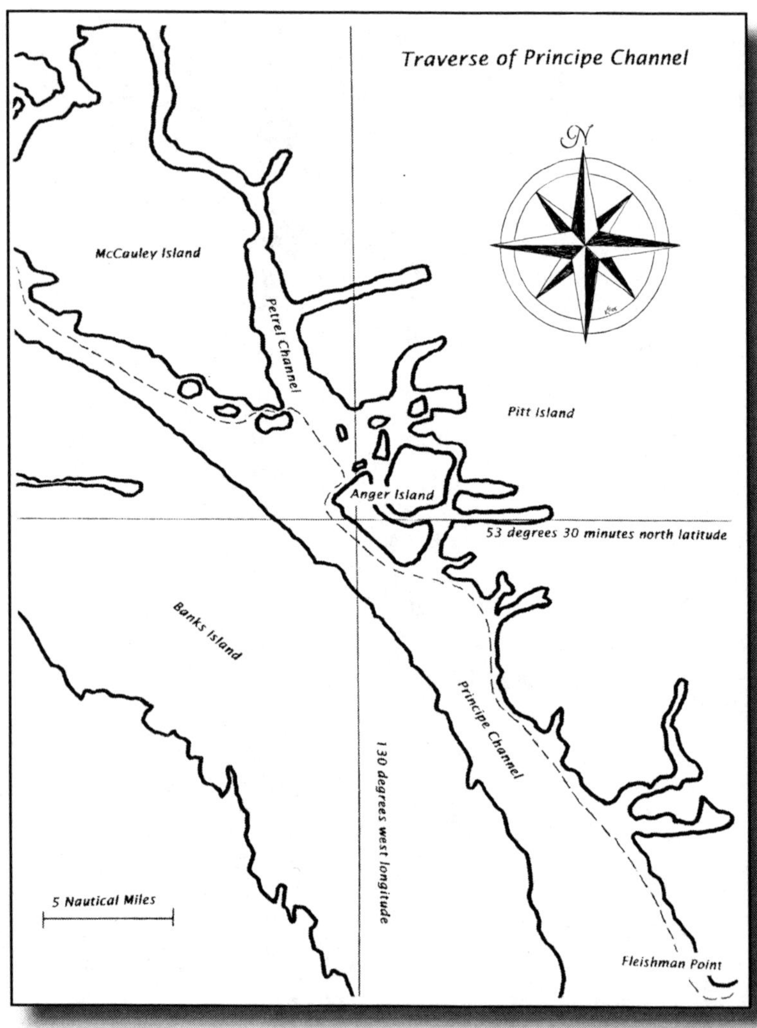
Traverse of Principe Channel
N
McCauley Island
Petrel Channel
Pitt Island
Anger Island
53 degrees 30 minutes north latitude
Banks Island
Principe Channel
130 degrees west longitude
5 Nautical Miles
Fleishman Point

SOUTH:

Into The Maw Of Principe

The decision-making styles employed by different folks are an interesting study. In most cases, our decisions are a concoction of logic, prior experience and intuition. However, we have learned from this trip and others that timing is a critical ingredient. Make the decision too early and the weather will change. Make the decision too late and the opportunity will be gone. The watchword is balance. Not too late, not too early, not too logical, not too intuitive.

You have three major options for travelling on water from Prince Rupert to Bella Bella. The first is the "Inside Passage," the ferry route running down Grenville and Princess Royal Channels. The second is the "half inside, half outside" passage, including Principe and Laredo

Channels, and the third option is the "outside," the true wild west coast, exposed to thousands of miles of open ocean. They each have their pro's and con's. Your decision must be based upon your skill at surf landings, tolerance of risk, the long-range weather forecast, and the opportunity for camps. Other considerations are the size of the group you're traveling in, the amount of fuel on hand for cooking with a portable stove, shipping hazards, your navigational ability, and the depth of your desire for isolation.

Our landing on McCauley that night was anything but graceful. I was definitely glad we had fibreglass and Kevlar beneath us instead of wood or canvas. We crashed ashore on round rocks the size of basketballs, and I winced as I heard cracking sounds from my overstressed hull. We jumped out as soon as we landed and hauled our boats out of danger, unable to help each other for fear of losing control of our individual kayaks. We used the surge of the surf to haul and scrape our way up the beach out of danger. The best you can do is hang onto the bow loop and wait until the surge lifts the 200-pound boat, then run and stumble as far as possible up the beach until the surf dumps it. You wait until it's lifted again and stumble up another few yards. McCauley camp had the most difficult access so far, and we were concerned abut subjecting them to such rough use.

After our mad scramble to safety we unloaded, did the carry, and I spent the next hour cutting the salal bushes to clear a tent space. Eventually, thanks to the pruning shears and hand chainsaw, an eight-by-eight patch appeared. The tent was now snug and secure, out of the wind.

The hand chainsaw was a fortuitous item. My daughter Sally had given it to me along with a book for my birthday. Had I known how useful it was to be, I would have included it when doing the early planning. I thanked her mentally every time we were faced with a solid wall of salal, especially when darkness was coming on and we'd had a rough landing. With the saw and pruning shears I could garden a tent pad in under an hour, and Sally's afterthought turned out to be a boon to our comfort.

At McCauley camp, Jaquie rustled up some tomato soup, bannock, and hot chocolate. Mmmm! Bread, the staple of the world – the chapatti of Nepal, the flatbread of the Southern States, and the "damper" of scout troops worldwide. We really took to bannock on these long trips. It lasts and lasts, it can be made with a variety of flavours or fillings, and it doesn't crush (especially the bannock I make). After sampling a bannock loaf I'd baked on a previous trip, my son Mark suggested rather undiplomatically that it would serve as a perfect hatch cover for my old Baidarka kayak. All I needed to do was cut a thread around the outside and it would screw right in, and probably be more watertight than the existing one!

That night, the food-hauling line was definitely not the regulation ten feet off the ground. In fact, our efforts were merely a feeble token. Any self-respecting bear would have laughed behind his paw and not even bothered to get off all fours to have a meal from this cache. However, it would have to do. We were bone weary, and fell asleep at eleven o'clock, just as the sun was going down. Our long summer solstice days punctuated with spectacular late evening sunsets resulted in shorter sleeping time.

In the morning we found our food cache still intact. We reversed the process of the night before, taking two hours to carry all our gear and empty boats down to the low tide line. Tide patterns advance about fifty minutes each day, and in the next few days the high tides would occur between one and four in the morning. We knew we would have to launch at low tide midmorning with long hauls, or get up in the dark. The third option was to launch on the afternoon high. On this particular morning we were away at ten o'clock on a rock-gouging, wave-crashing launch into a brighter day, and looking forward to what was clearly becoming the easiest part of our trip – the kayaking! On many an occasion I would hear Jaquie say, "Great, now we can relax on the water". After the rigours of the morning carry, we were always happy to slump in our kayak seats and revel in beauty on the way to our next camp.

Entering Principe Channel really gave us the feeling that we were making progress. We had seventy-eight miles behind us, with *only* five hundred and twenty-four to go. There were four days of southerly travel ahead, entirely within the channel of Principe. Soon after entering, we had our first opportunity to take a break while still making distance. A gently blowing nor'wester under a crystal clear sky provided both inspiration and impetus. We rafted our boats together, put up the tarp between our paddles and ran under sail against the flood for the next four miles.

There are various methods of sailing a kayak. They fall into two broad categories, engineered and jury-rigged. Engineered methods involve a stepped mast, a tailored sail (usually triangular) and various deck fittings to secure the sheets. We use the jury-rigged method for its simplicity, as it uses equipment standard for a kayak with no extra technology. With the boats rafted together, each of us holds one end of our working paddles between our legs – more or less vertically, but slightly angled outside the kayaks. Over the top blades we make the tarp taut by pulling down on the tie lines at its corners.

This forms a primitive fifty square-foot lugsail that can really pull the boats along fast on a downwind run. Because the boats are rafted together, the whole rig is quite stable. Steering is achieved by one paddler operating the rudder in sync with the other paddler. If the gusts get too strong, it's an easy matter to let go of the sheets and spill the wind. The next four miles flashed past in well under an hour while we enjoyed the scenery, the eagles, and a chat in the warm sun. Wilderness travel's pretty good, we thought, especially after the tough camp we'd had on McCauley the night before.

Jaquie:

Sailing! What exhilaration – to fly along with the wind after the two-hour long, grungy slog to load and launch this morning. I was quite nervous as Rick showed me how to rig the tarp and paddles, but his quiet competence and boundless patience soon quieted my fears. We gazed up at the deep blue of the sky, watched the tarp fill and strain with the wind as we raised the paddles, then grinned at one another when the boats began to pick up speed. My arms tired in time, so we lowered the sail and chattered while we stowed the tarp and got out a snack to celebrate. Sometime later we spied a grand spot where we pulled up and sunned ourselves dry, along with the tent and our damp clothing.

When we are asked if we travelled down the Inside Passage, it is difficult to answer. There are several "inside" and "outside" passages. For example, the ferry system uses Grenville and Princess Royal Channels, the furthest east beneath the mountains of the Coast Range. Another, roughly parallel series of passages winds its way south. This route is sometimes inside, and sometimes breaks out into areas that are exposed to the Pacific. Principe and Petrel Channels are examples. Protected passages up and down the coast usually have excellent shelter from the big Pacific swells, but offer few camp sites and very damp firewood. The camps are found in thick forest or salal thickets, and are extremely difficult to access because there is a wall of rock as much as fifteen feet high to be negotiated before landing. But the inside route does have a quiet, spiritual beauty of its own, and attracts many travellers.

Travel on the outside is breathtakingly beautiful, with clean, clear waters, great fishing, spectacular whale encounters, and long sandy beaches between headlands. This route is strewn with "boomers", or heavy seas that break over underwater rocks and reefs. Surge channels provide endless excitement in a scene that's wild, boisterous and constantly moving. However, good surf-landing techniques are a must to reach camps, and often a kayaker must travel many hours without being able to land. Leaving camp in the morning usually involves a surf-launch that requires a special technique to avoid getting a cockpit full of water.

Another discomfort encountered on the outside is sand. In the city we fantasize about beautiful sandy beaches and soaking up the rays. The exposed outside has to be one of the most beautiful environments on earth, but ask any kayaker who travels there and you will probably hear about sand, loud and long. Sand eventually makes its way into absolutely everything – into toothpaste, food, paddle shafts, stoves, eyes, ears, sleeping bags, and journals. It grinds its way everywhere as if its only mission in life is to penetrate small cracks and orifices. When I once asked a couple who'd spent three months circumnavigating Vancouver Island what their biggest discomfort had been, their reply in unison had been, "Sand! We'll be happy if we never see another grain of sand as long as we live!"

Principe Channel is about fifty miles long. We navigated the first thirteen miles of it that day. We even spent a couple of wonderful hours at Logan Bay, sunbathing and drying out the tent. Just as we were remarking that we hadn't seen any shipping traffic for days, within half an hour, two cruise ships and a tug towing a barge passed up the channel. As I lay like a lizard on a warm rock, idly eyeing the ships, Jaquie reacted. She yelled, "The wake!" We catapulted upright and streaked down fifty yards of rocks to the water to save our precious boats from being pounded by the wash from the ships – all in full view of hundreds of tourists lining the rail to catch a glimpse of local wildlife. Perhaps home videos on living room walls in Frankfurt and Yokohama are amusing audiences with two crazy Canadians in the "altogether". What an ad for BC Tourism!

The peace of our sunbathing was shattered, and our perfect day was ageing, so we moved on and started looking for a camp. Within a very short time, the *perfect camp* appeared – a dead calm landing, a beach full of dry, bleached driftwood, a rocky peninsula at just the right angle for us to watch the sunset, a bottle of red wine to complement an excellent meal. Eleven o'clock to bed in the fading shades of sunset with the sound of the ocean gently washing the shore. *All's right in our world.* Needless to say, in our journals this place is fondly named "Camp Ideal."

The dawn competed with the glory of the previous night's sunset, the fading stars gradually giving way to pastels as first light grew in the East. Leaving "Camp Ideal" at seven-thirty, our launch was an easy slide off the logs into deep, crystal clear water. I remember feeling strong and completely integrated with the natural environment that morning, with the feeling of living in the day, and for the moment. No tomorrow, no yesterday. *Man, this is happiness. Now I know why I'm here and why I do this.*

This day became the longest of our trip, covering twenty-one miles. We were feeling fit and had a relatively easy traverse, crossing the southern end of Petrel Channel to Anger Island in the morning calm. For this part of the coast I had a nine-mile gap between two of my large-scale (1:40,000) charts, bridged only by a small-scale (1:250,000) chart, so we lacked detail of the shoreline.

Being accustomed to reading the series of charts like random pages in a book, I missed the details of the story unfolding. We relied on chart and magnetic compass for our navigation, but compass bearings are somewhat inaccurate when taken from a rolling kayak. I navigated with one eye on the compass needle and the other on the horizon for balance. Bearings become even less accurate when using a small-scale chart. We experienced no problems but this chart gave me the feelings I get when I unrope after a climb – naked and vulnerable.

Reality jolted me when I considered how the ancient peoples had traversed this coast for thousands of years with just the information they gleaned from the stories of others. Perhaps they had a primitive "chart" consisting of a notched stick of a particular shape, showing the shoreline and its main features.

How they negotiated the big tidal rapids and multiple channels of this remote coast I'll never know, but they survived!

Before we'd embarked on our trip, a non-kayaker had asked, "Why do you need charts? Why don't you just follow the shoreline?" This is a reasonable question from one who visualizes the coast as a series of beaches, neatly lined up end-to-end from north to south. We knew that merely following the shoreline would take us up the many fiords that cut deep into the Coast Range, and that we would inevitably take a wrong turn and end up travelling many miles before coming back to where we'd started. To illustrate, if you followed the coastline of the inland sea feeding the Nakwakto Rapids from the mouth of Slingsby Channel and out again, you would cover more than twice the distance from Alaska to Vancouver, just within that inlet. Good charts are a must.

After rolling out of our sleeping bags early this morning, and paddling for four hours, our reward, while lounging in warm sunshine on Anger Island, was a breakfast of granola and fruit. Despite glancing about with curiosity, we didn't see the hermit who is purported to live there.

Our route now took us around Foul Point, and on down Principe Channel with a break at "Penny's Beach" for our lunch. Long daylight hours at these latitudes enabled us to do extended mileage with little effort by breaking our daily journey into several smaller stints. Canned salmon and beans tasted fine to a pair of weary, utterly content travellers at "Penny's Camp" a few miles farther on. We slipped into our sleeping bags at eleven.

Jaquie:

Many little gems of experience are scattered through each day, many poignant, others just everyday events that, in this environment, seem more significant. I have lost the cap that Larry gave me just before we boarded the ferry at Port Hardy, and feel bad about my carelessness.

> *Today I glided silently over a bed of plumose anemones in a narrow channel. I imagined a certain bonhomie in their gently waving tentacles, and I marvelled at the elaborate, detailed painting of the face and plumage of a harlequin duck. In the palette of colours, we detected dark blue, grey, metallic blue, chestnut and dark brown – with patches of colour delineated by lines of white and black. We paddled toward a flock of small black diving birds with whiteish beaks – perhaps scoters. As we approached to within a few metres, the closest ones dove, resurfacing at a distance they must have thought safe. How good to be able to live among these marvellous creatures, sharing their world without doing them any harm.*

As I drifted toward sleep, I thought of Victoria Jason who had soloed the Northwest Passage by kayak. I once asked her about her daily mileage on that North Slope trip and had been surprised when she'd replied, "Often I would cover forty miles in a day." With long Arctic hours of daylight and no reason to stop, the miles fly by while travelling solo. Although well south of the Arctic Circle, daylight hours were long, and to some degree we experienced a similar phenomenon.

We wilderness travellers view darkness as a barrier between periods of daylight. Our previous mental conditioning determines that movement comes to a halt at dark. We stop, set up camp, trading the travelling mode for a residential one. Contrary to this habit, some of my extreme outdoor friends can ignore night and day. They eat when hungry, sleep in a bivvy sack when tired, and move on when rested. Many extreme Arctic and Antarctic journeys function like this. It's simply a different way of looking at life. Night need not be the barrier we might think.

June twenty-seventh must have been the toughest day of the trip for Jaquie. It rained hard as we prepared to launch, turning the rocks greasy with seaweed and mud. Slippery, unstable footing compounded by the extra low tide led to a treacherous carry.

As we carried my empty boat down the rocks, Jaquie led with her left arm wrapped around the front keel, the bow tucked close to her left side. We made our wobbly way over logs, around patches of slippery kelp. Next moment I saw her legs go out from under her on the rocks. She crashed onto the kayak and stayed down, motionless for a long moment. It was obvious something was very wrong. This woman normally bounces right back up and keeps going.

My first thought was a broken forearm. She had gone down directly on top of a football-sized rock. With a jumble of fears racing through my head, I put down the stern. Due to the topography of the coastline, we hadn't been able to pick up a weather forecast for two days, so it was unlikely we'd be able to get a distress message out on my VHF radio. A myriad of possibilities, obstacles, and challenges tumbled around in my head. My adrenaline pumped. The trip suddenly changed from an idyllic yesterday to a desperate today.

As I struggled over the rocks to her, she pulled her hand out from beneath the boat. Fortunately, the rock wasn't too jagged, and she escaped with just a badly bruised and scraped hand. But this was the least of our troubles, as it became obvious the more severe injury was a cracked rib. I suggested we call off the launch and wait for as long as it took to solve the problem, but Jaquie is one tough lady! After exploring the rib and hand, she quietly and calmly decided we should push on as normal. It would all get better in its own time. Years of wilderness travel experiences probably combine to prepare a person mentally to carry on under duress.

Jaquie:

My day has not started well. Everything seems to take longer in the rain. It has turned the seaweed and lichen into treacherous ambushes. Two hours after high tide we packed the gear down across the rocks to the least lumpy bit of foreshore. After the gear came my little Ruby Red Boat. Rick and I cringe each time we have to drag our boats over the barnacled rocks, so we often spend some time combing the high tide line for round, rolly bits of driftwood to skid the hulls over the worst ones. Unfortunately, this beach seemed devoid of the wood of choice.

Rick usually carries the heavy stern end of his boat, and I lead with the bow. The most comfortable position for me to carry seems to be standing as straight as possible with the bow tucked up on my hip, one arm around it, the other free for balance.

Not so balanced this morning, it appears. One foot went right, the other went left, and down we crashed, Seafarer and I, onto the rocks. Stunned disbelief, then anger and pain danced around me. First I pulled my hand from under the boat. Knuckles a bit bashed up, but no fracture. Fingers work. Ribs are the worst – how could I have been so clumsy and jeopardized the trip?

After the surprise wears off, I'm gradually able to convince Rick that we should push on. Now the tide has retreated even further, but somehow I'm on the water with little recollection of the final carry or launch.

Still raining. There is lots of intertidal life on the rocky walls. We putter along, examining colonies of tiny black mussels being munched by beautiful orange and green turret snails.

The sea is very still under a low, wet sky and sets my mood for the day. Rick is very good about letting me muddle along muttering to myself. Somewhere along the way I have decided to slow down and take better care of my body. Tonight our tent is up under the trees beside a little waterfall that patters into a beautiful mossy pool.

With fresh water aplenty, there is the luxury of a warm wash in fresh, rather than salty, water! It is heavenly to crawl into the tent feeling clean.

Our day proceeded just a bit slower than normal, and I winced every time Jaquie lifted or hauled gear. It would be another twenty-eight days before the rib healed to the point where pain was minimal. Surprising as it seemed, normal paddling was relatively kind to the injured rib, even in a heavy swell. The painful part was in choppy waves, especially when the waves were reflected off the rocks. I would often see her heading out to sea, well clear of headlands, to paddle in the rhythmic waves that were running free, clear of obstacles. She wore her wetsuit every day now, with a fleece under it to provide firm support for her trunk to minimize the painful lumps and bumps.

It rained continuously throughout 'broken rib day,' but the sea remained calm. Five porpoises passed us going the other way, seals with their pups were hauled up on rocky islets, harlequin ducks paddled around the inlets, and we saw the occasional mink running along logs on the beach.

We were now 120 miles en route, but had just covered 108 miles of our originally- planned track. Physically and mentally, we were stronger now, solidly immersed in the rhythm of packing, eating up the miles, unpacking, putting up camp, cooking, hauling food up the 'bear' tree, sleeping, and repeating the whole process day after day.

Apart from the rib injury, our main health challenges were in managing small wounds. Barnacle cuts, rubs, scrapes, and blisters were extremely difficult to treat and slow to heal because of the constant saltwater immersion. Most mornings we would spend half an hour in the tent after waking, treating these minor scrapes. We tried drying them, applying cream to them, leaving them open, dressing them, and all combinations of the above. Hands and feet suffered the greatest damage. No dressing stayed on for any length of time. We tried several brands of supposedly "waterproof" dressings, duct tape, bandannas, and bandages. Some that were reputed to be the best were off before we could get aboard the boats. Our best strategy appeared to be drying the wound at night and using Elastoplast bandages during travel hours. The thick fabric and generous coating of gum on the sticky side lasted for most of the day.

The constant rubbing on the paddle shafts caused callouses on our hands. This provided nature's best protection against blisters. A discomfort and annoyance was the Neoprene rash we experienced after wearing wetsuits for long hours. The options were to wear thin polypropelene clothing under the wetsuit, defeating the purpose of the suit, or wear nothing under it and get a rash. Somehow on this journey we could accept all this as part of the game, and it didn't worry us unduly.

Late in the day we searched for a camp we knew of in an inlet named, for some reason we have yet to discover, Port Stephens. We saw no sign of human hand, and certainly no evidence to suggest it had ever served as a port. I fantasized about pizza as I paddled along in the rain, salivating at the thought of rich tomato sauce and melted cheese, making ridiculous suggestions that we radio the Coast Guard to order up our favourite Vegetarian Deluxe, and then conjecturing how long it would take to arrive. We made camp at Port Stephens, and drifted into our usual routines. While I gathered firewood, Jaquie dammed and diverted a tiny creek that was trickling through the only spot flat enough for a kitchen. Once the water had been channeled away from our little beach, and the gravel had a chance to dry, we put the tarp up, and Jaquie disappeared under it while I wrestled with lighting a fire in the pouring rain.

I must have worked on the fire for nearly an hour before it was anything like self-sustaining, all the while vaguely wondering what Jaquie was doing under the tarp. Suddenly she appeared with – you guessed it – a perfect thin-crust pizza, topped with mozzarella and cheddar cheese, sun-dried tomatoes and tuna, accompanied by fresh-from-the-oven cornbread. This smelled like only fresh cornbread and pizza can smell. I thought it was a dream. A *second* pizza from the oven filled not only our tummies but our spirits. All this after bucketing rain, a cracked rib, a hard day's paddling, and diverting a creek. Master chef Jaquie, what a winner!

Before falling asleep, we rounded off the evening with a backgammon game in the tent. In so many ways, what an amazing day.

Jaquie:

Villages are favourite foraging spots for feathered scavengers as well as for bears. These birds congregate on beaches or near garbage cans – wherever they can smell discarded food. When cheeky black crows or haughty ravens come calling on our camp, we look at beaks and tails to discern who is who. "Crow," I will hoot. "Square tail!" Or, Rick will announce, "Listen to the croak. Must be a raven somewhere over us." Head swivelling about, binoculars coming out, he will confirm the diamond-shaped tail, indicating our visitor is a raven. We marvel at the repertoire of rattles, squawks, chitters, and bongs when they speak to us of secrets in the forest and on the shore. We feel like intruders in their domain, unwelcome voyeurs who have disturbed the natural order of life here. These shiny black guardians of the unknown are a curious lot. They approach our camp warily when we are in sight, but we have little doubt that if we wander away to scout the far end of a beach or to walk around a point, they will be quick to carry off any shiny bit of gear or food left unattended.

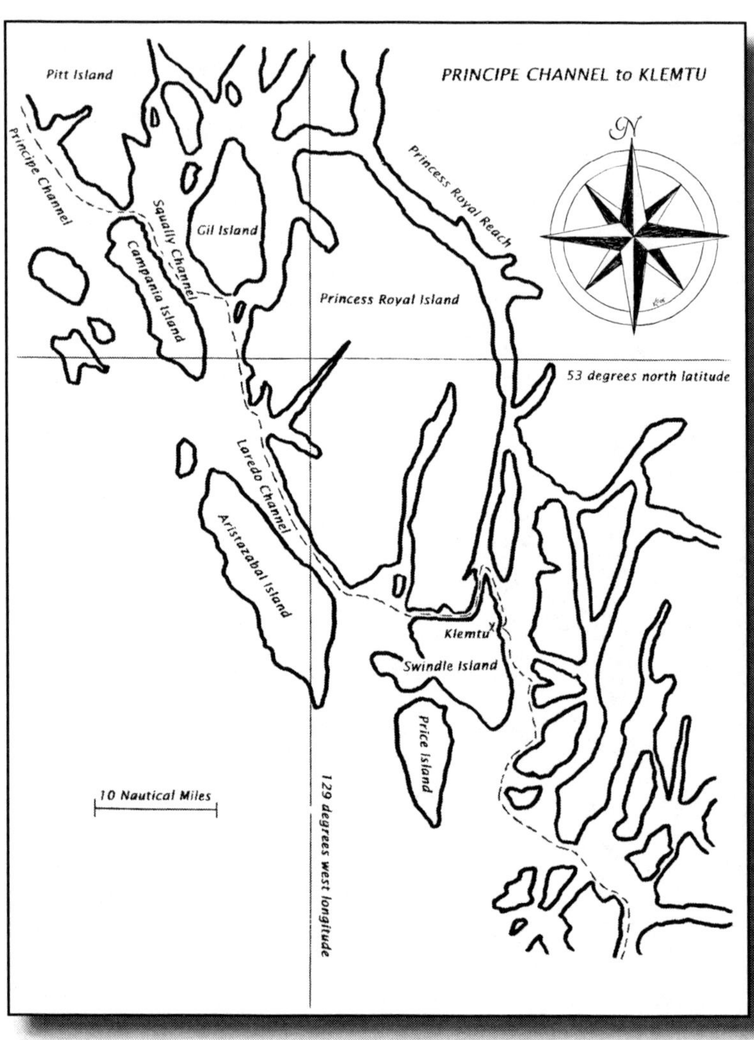
PRINCIPE CHANNEL to KLEMTU
Pitt Island
Principe Channel
Squally Channel
Gil Island
Campania Island
Princess Royal Reach
Princess Royal Island
N
53 degrees north latitude
Loredo Channel
Aristazabal Island
Klemtu
Swindle Island
Price Island
10 Nautical Miles
129 degrees west longitude

Exit:

Southeast From Principe

We all fear the unknown. But we kayakers have our own set of fears. We look at charts of unfamiliar narrows and rapids and wonder: How fast does it run? Will there be a refuge? What is the exposure? Are there reefs and boomers? Can we get through the surge channels? What other challenges could appear? Can we forage or catch fish if we run short of food?

I recall sitting on my father's knee when I was four years old and him telling me a story about a soldier who ran twenty-six miles from Marathon to Athens. He told me about people who to this day run a twenty-six mile race called a marathon. As a small boy I wondered how anyone could possibly run and keep on running for that mighty distance. They must surely be super mortals. As a

child, the unknown and the unfamiliar made me wide-eyed and excited.

Thirty-three years later, seven years after my father's death, I found myself running my first marathon. On crossing the finish line I didn't feel at all like a super mortal. I felt damned good, but I just felt like an ordinary guy who'd committed to the task and had trained hard. I didn't feel really different at all. Now, it's the Ironman that seems like an impossible feat.

We humans always seem to be looking onward and upward to something bigger and better. There's nothing really wrong with this, but perhaps we should pause, look back for a moment of reflection, and occasionally be content with past accomplishments.

When we left Principe Channel, it felt like saying good-bye to an old friend. We looked back, and it left us with a good feeling. What had at first been unfamiliar had become a haven.

We learn to push the limits, increment by increment, not by leaps and bounds, not blindly. In doing so, we minimize the risk of injury or worse. It all depends on personal tolerance of risk. But when we get to a feeling of comfort with the familiar, we should pause for a moment to enjoy our environment before we move on.

We're up and at it again, in the rain. Five and a half hours into the teeth of the southerly and we're finally out of Principe Channel and around Fleishman Point. We've seen Principe in the rain, in the wind, and under the brilliant summer sun. It provided us salmon for sustenance and safe havens for snug nights. Now as we're leaving it behind, I wonder if we'll be back this way some day.

Fleishman Point provided us with some strenuous paddling through the current, but the effort rewarded us with a sheltered camp. Pulling onto the shingle beach we saw a temporary structure consisting of a tarp frame and a fireplace, obviously well-used over the years by numerous travellers moving up and down the coast. By the time we landed, the sun had come out and all had been transformed into the kind of kayaking we love. A dry, warm tent site, a pleasant beach where we could dry ourselves and our gear in the sunshine. A supper of chicken, gravy, and sautéed yams, followed by a good night's sleep. Our small lagoon was quiet and peaceful, and we spent time watching the bird and animal life along the shore.

After a dry and comfortable night, we set off again at nine-fifteen with an easy launch on the high tide from a calm shingle beach. What a treat! We never cease to be amazed at the wide range of conditions within a few short miles of coastline. One moment it's hard survival; the next can be sheer bliss.

Slipping out of the lagoon we crossed the two-mile wide Otter Channel to the north end of Campania Island. Campania has unique topography. We agreed it reminded us of the Scottish moors or the Lakes District in the British Isles. At the highest elevations, in the sub-alpine tundra, worn grey rocks were interpersed with low growth of heathers and tough-looking grasses. We found that the east side had fewer landings and beaches than the west side. Campania is very different from the surrounding fiords and islands that are green, lush, and heavily forested. We are keen to return here one day to camp, explore, and climb to the top of Mt. Pender to view the numerous fiord-like inlets that lead to inland lakes. The karst, or limestone formation is tough and compelling to climbers and scramblers, and I can tell Jaquie's fingers are itching to explore the warm rock routes.

We rounded Fanny Point, taking advantage of the flood down the west side of Squally Channel, and then crossed to the Skinner Islands, having no notion of the treat that was in store for us. Our track took us close to Gil Island, and suddenly a vertical plume of spray indicated a whale only half a mile ahead. As the tail flukes rose and fell a couple of times, we snapped off a few photos from a distance, excited to just see a whale.

Another half mile along we rounded the Skinner Islands, and there was the whale again! It rose and showed its back a little closer this time, so we drifted to watch it feeding with a regular six minutes down and then three blows on the surface before diving again. We were in wonder at a creature this huge. How, with amazing navigation senses, it could manoeuvre in the shallows and reefs around the islands without grounding itself. At last, it submerged and stayed down for a long time.

Our kayaks drifted slowly towards a white sandy beach with definite possibilities for a camp. Jaquie speculated that our big, grey friend had rounded the island, but something told me we should wait just a little longer. Suddenly and silently, within a boat length of Jaquie's kayak, the enormous wet back with its small dorsal fin broke the surface, arched, and was followed by the tail majestically rising, then slipping back into the water, with a cascade of droplets streaming off the flukes. Jaquie, still poised with her camera in her hands, ran off shot after shot as fast as it would advance. The mirror-like calm of Squally Channel made a perfect backdrop for one of the best whale picture sequences we have.

We had kayaked with whales before, but this experience was certainly the most breathtaking. When a whale surfaces in front of such a frail craft, with the bulk of this gentle creature right beneath, it feels akin to watching an avalanche thunder past. We feel tiny, vulnerable, awestruck – but totally enraptured to the point of being unafraid.

Afterwards I played "What-if" in my head. What if that creature was having a bad day and decided to give our boats a nudge? What if it chose to whack its tail on us to see what a flat kayak would look like? We never follow, search out, or molest the creatures of the ocean, and encourage others to let wildlife go about its business in peace, but sometimes wild creatures appear before us as if they wish to experience us. With no choice in the encounter, being quiet and still allows us a truly magical experience. As we watched the whale systematically work its way across the bay feeding, there was little doubt in our minds that it was keeping an eye on us as it left us behind.

The afternoon was drawing to a close, so we ran our boats into the beach that we had observed previously. 'Whale View Camp' turned out to be another in our list of best camps on the coast. Bumblebees and hummingbirds were in abundance, the steep beach provided us with an all-tide landing, and the southerly aspect gave us a warm, pleasant spot for observing the sunset, and enjoying a glass of wine with our pasta.

Jaquie:

The green, wet bush provides limited forage for wild pollinators such as bumblebees, leafcutter bees, and hummingbirds. Salal thickets are everywhere, wild roses abound on a few dry, sunny beach verges, but due to their short blossoming period, the blooms which produce the nectar and pollen essential for bees are in short supply. In researching habitat for bumblebees, I have read that they favour areas with higher-than-average rainfall. That doesn't explain to me why they appear along the edges of snow patches in sub-alpine areas in spring. Often as we paddle just offshore, we are circled by big, fuzzy bees and we assume that they are attracted by the bright colours of our boats, clothing, or gear. Surely they can't mistake our 'fragrance' for that of flowers! Many times we hear the loud buzz of their approach before we see them, and puzzle at how they find us. Do they spot us from the distant beach and make a special trip to reconnoitre, or do they forage from island to island continuously? I know that they are able to travel long distances, because I once read of a lone bumblebee sighted 28 kilometres from land, apparently heading in a straight line from the Tasman Peninsula to Bruny Island, just south of Australia.

Each spring hummingbirds make an annual migration

from their wintering grounds in Central America and Mexico to parts of the United States and Canada. The spring migration lasts until May or early June when these marathon flyers arrive in the northern United States and Canada. We were delighted to see these tiny birds hovering over our heads here on the beaches in June. Our colourful gear seems to act as a great lure for flower-loving critters. We often hear them before we see them, partly because we sit facing the sea, not the foliage behind us where they hover for cover. During rapid flight, male broad-tailed hummingbirds such as the rufous produce a particularly shrill, buzzing whistle as air rushes through slots created by the tips of their primary wing feathers. These tiny birds have evolved marvellous adaptations to their environment. They migrate thousands of miles to follow the annual flowering seasons, burning enormous calories. Consequently, they must eat twelve to fifteen times each hour to power their little bodies, but can lower their night-time body temperature to conserve energy. I think our body temperature must drop at night too. Some mornings I feel pretty cold when crawling out of the tent, and only warm up with a bit of brisk exercise or a hot meal.

Although we always note the nectar they require as a carbohydrate, we forget that they catch spiders and small insects for the protein needed to build the bodies of their young. Females use spider silk and moss as materials for a tight, soft nest for their families. This coast certainly provides the moss in great quantities, and in the cool mornings we see the spiders' webs stretched in the bush, glittering with dew.

Today is the last day of June. We launched after a pancake breakfast and although Jaquie was delighting in the hot sun, she soon had her line in the water, her fishing instinct indicating that the time, current and location was right. Sure enough, she caught a good-sized spring salmon off Fawcett Point where the current flushed abundant nutrients around the rocky tip. Small fish abounded in these waters, the principal food for the predatory salmon that are a step higher on the marine food chain. She cleaned the fish at sea, washed herself and the boat down thoroughly, and secured the catch across her deck to take home for our supper. Occasionally we splashed water on the fish to keep it moist.

We crossed Whale Channel to Ashdown Island, took a short break, and then really poured on the power against a vicious southerly beam sea to reach Princess Royal Island on the far side of Casanave Passage. The crossing was rough enough for us to be slapped hard on the starboard side, forcing us to apply some aggressive bracing upwind just to stay upright. By the time we reached Princess Royal, the southerly was really building up. We inched our way down the west coast to Duckers Island, thankful to be tucked into shelter for the night behind the islands. We named the secluded white sand beach 'Otter Camp' due to the family of river otters continually swimming to and fro between the reefs, fishing with what appeared to be playful abandon.

With the regular housekeeping done, our salmon was wrapped in aluminum foil, and the fire was built. As soon as the fire burned hot enough, into the coals went the succulent treat. The sun came out and the wind died. We spent a quiet evening sitting on our log watching the half moon until we fell asleep about midnight.

Jaquie:

Sunny mornings are blissful, and I am filled with a joyous sense of well-being. Perhaps I am the reincarnation of an Aztec or Mayan sun-worshipper, as I take every opportunity to lift my face, bare my skin, and soak up the heat and light. This morning on the water is no excep-

tion as I strip off my shirt, and roll down my spray skirt to indulge myself while I fish. Hooking a 3 to 4 pound spring salmon (small for its species, but just right for us) was exhilarating, but cleaning it on my deck proved to be fairly messy. It took more time to clean the fish, the boat deck, and myself than it did to hook it, play it and land it. Satisfaction and pride are warming my insides as much as the sun on my outside. When the wind rose, the sunbathing ended, and I returned to a semblance of respectability in time to chat with a few resort fishermen with their guides from the nearby King Pacific Lodge and West Coast Resorts.

July 1st, Canada Day! Into the water we went at 10:15 and round the point toward Emily Carr Inlet, roaring out our best rendition of "O Canada." No wonder we saw no seals for a while!

Emily Carr Inlet conjured visions of deep mysterious forest, stately dark evergreens, with perhaps a cabin hiding in shadows. British Columbians are proud of this renowned Canadian artist who, influenced somewhat by the style of the Group of Seven in Eastern Canada, evoked the power and glory of our rugged coast. But the reality of the landscape shocked us. The inlet was dominated by a huge clearcut. What a travesty to the memory of Emily Carr! We had paddled past old growth forests for weeks, and this hit us as a complete surprise.

Deeply disappointed, we hurried away in a two-foot chop, through the Sager Islands across the mouth of Surf Inlet. Although we had no trouble with this crossing, inlets exiting to the west can produce big standing waves on an ebb tide in opposition to a westerly wind. Our wind now was southeasterly so the crossing was a little lumpy. However, the wind direction persisted for the next four days – all the way across Camano Sound, down Laredo Channel, and across Laredo Sound, a distance of thirty-four hard-won miles.

As we slogged our way southwards into the wind and down the west coast of Princess Royal Island, my body went on autopilot, and my mind began to roam. *Could this be a defensive mechanism dulling muscular stress when the laws of physics are working against me?*

In a reverie, I travelled back to my first sea kayak trip off the West Coast of Vancouver Island in the early eighties. My training for this experience amounted to an hour in a rental kayak in False Creek in Vancouver two days before leaving on the trip. Starting from Tofino, we paddled up the outside of Vargas Island, to Flores Island. My travelling companions were far more experienced than I, so I blindly followed through all sorts of sea states in an old West Greenland kayak that didn't even have a rudder. Back then, 'real' kayakers supposedly didn't use rudders. I've since learned differently, and my comfort level has risen.

The trip definitely offered a steep learning curve, and I came to believe it was perfectly normal to put up with 20 knots of wind in four-foot breaking waves on top of a fifteen-foot Pacific swell. Enjoyment wasn't a part of the experience at all, and I frequently suffered a surge of adrenaline, followed by a bad attack of dry mouth, a condition closely associated with severe contraction of the lower sphincter muscle, and wide eyes. The brain signals clearly that you are close to that thin red line. Adventurers who have been to the edge, and experienced this will relate it to a good time. On that trip I accepted the conditions as normal – I simply didn't know any better.

Now, sixteen years later, and paddling my third boat, I feel so much more relaxed and attuned to the changing conditions. The marine environment is now as much 'home' to me as anywhere. Despite the heavy water breaking over my bow and occasionally slapping me in the chest, I felt confident and relaxed. I pondered upon this comfort level, and came to the conclusion it was due to total control over whether I stayed ashore or put to sea. *I could choose!* This was unlike the first trip where I was relying on the judgment of experienced friends, and was determined not to let them down.

My present attitude has nothing to do with being more courageous or willing to take greater risks. In fact, my safety margins increase as years slip by. I am, however, more comfortable with my judgment. Judgment gives me a sound basis for making the go / no-go decision, allows me to stay on the beach while others go. I trust logic and judgment as opposed to emotional decision-making. This new attitude even allows me to be called "chicken" and consider it a compliment. The wonderful thing about our long journey is feeling no pressure to go anywhere, locked into a destination or a deadline. We will shelter from a storm for a week if necessary, and it won't make any difference in the world. We will *live* on the coast, *be* nomadic inhabitants of the shoreline, *experience* this lifestyle.

This is vastly different from the 'eco-challenge' philosophy that drives a team with the bare minimum of equipment to reach the end as fast as possible, relying on outside logistics and emergency response by flipping a button on an EPIRB (Emergency Position Indicator Radio Beacon) to activate a whole search and rescue system. We'd decided during the planning stages that the 'Jaquie and Rick Marine Rescue Service' would be our best resource.

Suddenly, a larger-than-normal wave slewed my kayak off course and I was back again – Canada Day, 2001. The seas were rising, and in reply to a question from Jaquie, I yelled over the wind, "Well, put it this way, there's no way I would launch in these conditions if I was leading a guided party!"

Running through a small reef, we pulled up on a steep rocky beach in the lee of a headland sheltered from the gale, and spent some time examining campsite possibilities. This had become a habit at most rest stops, one that would prove to be of great value eventually. In time, the wind moderated, and off we went again, thrashing around the headland and paddling four exhausting miles along cliffs with no landing whatsoever. The one and only respite we found was Evinrude Inlet. Here we found a narrow beach with a rocky landing, and the evening carry began.

We could do this well-practised routine in silence; we had no need to communicate verbally. Bags would emerge from the hatches, hauling them up the beach would begin. When boats and gear were up above the high tide line, I offered Jaquie the 'gift' of a night off, something we do for each other from time to time during our trips. There is no schedule or plan to this. One or the other of us will spontaneously take over the work of making camp, preparing dinner and doing chores. The resting person can read a book, have a snooze, or sit on the beach with a glass of wine until supper is served. Sometimes even a massage gets thrown in as part of the deal. Jaquie looked grateful for a chance to loaf and recharge her batteries, and I set myself to the tasks.

Cutting a tent space out of the bush was our only choice in this deep ravine, and we were aware that our tent was bridging an animal trail. Jaquie had crawled in for a nap before supper. In the damp and drizzle I decided against building a fire. It was getting late, we were both very hungry, and firewood was scarce.

As I puttered about lighting the stove, I glanced around from time to time up the ravine and at the steep bank in front of me. There, from only ten metres up the sidehill, gleamed a pair of dark, intelligent eyes focused clearly upon me through the salal bushes. I reached for the bear spray thinking, "Well, It's not a very *big* grizzly." The animal turned, still partly hidden, and I thought, "Would a young moose be in terrain like this?" Then it moved into view. I realized we had a wolf in camp. With my quiet announcement of company, Jaquie came out of the tent in a hurry to gaze with me in awe at this beautiful, grizzled black and grey creature.

We three contemplated each other for what seemed an age. Then, with no hurry or sign of fear, it moved quietly up the gully behind the tent. With my energy revived from this encounter, I threw myself into building a fire – extremely motivated.

While supper cooked we brewed a big pot of tea so our bladders would be up to the task of marking the territory round our camp. Between checking the fire and organizing the meal, I built a barrier out of salal on the animal trail behind the tent, and thoroughly 'marked' that as well. Later in the tent we chuckled about Farley Mowat and his example in his book *Never Cry Wolf.*

Jaquie:

Canada Day! How appropriate to be living so close to our environment on this day, the 1st of July. I feel more a part of what Canada means to me than I ever could have imagined. Our days are a long chain of calendar photos, and although I carry my camera on my deck, I don't even try to capture it all: the slippery bits of magic in the cloud, the wind patterns across the water as a squall approaches, the dark line of trees we drift under as we wind in and out of the little bays and inlets. The tide slides the water down the wet rocks too fast for the snails and sea stars to follow, and we glimpse life on a horizontal plane, with a window into the complex pattern of lives we paddle above all day, every day.

Today, there was a little sun through the clouds now and then, and the wind was making us work a bit as we crossed Surf Inlet at slack tide. After six miles we took a break to strategize. Rick quietly rigged his boat to tow me if necessary. My jaw feels a bit tight – that stubborn streak is showing, and I am determined to keep going as long as I can without being silly about it. But my chest and back are very sore today.

After another four miles we made Evinrude Channel and a rocky little camp with a tiny spot in the salal across a game path for the tent. Rick gardened the spot a bit and stacked the prunings up the trail to alert any animals to our presence in their neighbourhood.

My best buddy gave me a night off, inviting me to have a rest while he made dinner. What a treat. In the tent, I set up our beds and eased myself down and closed my eyes, thoughts wandering as the aches and pains introduced themselves again. Then Rick coughed his 'Alpha Male Cough' and announced, "We have a wolf in camp!" I stood quietly beside Rick until our visitor had retreated into the gully behind the tent.

While meandering along the high tide line I discovered a clump of tall, lily-like blackish-brown flowers. My instincts tell me they are chocolate lilies, but I have only seen them in dryer areas in the interior, never on the shore. I took notes and a photo for later confirmation. I have discovered the loss of my pocketknife, and mourn the loss of an old and dear companion on many a foray into the wilderness.

The night passed peacefully, and we slept soundly. The following morning it was raining heavily on Wolf Camp, so I rigged the tarp and searched for firewood. Just in against the ravine wall we found the wolf's den, deep beneath the roots of a tree. It appeared to have been used often, judging by the well-worn trail at the entrance. Was it a 'resting den' while commuting for food or a 'watching den' along a fresh water seep where game might come to drink? If it had been a 'family den,' the wolf might have had much more to say about our presence. We launched on the high slack at 11:15, back to the battle of the southeaster down Laredo Channel, now against the ebb in addition to the wind.

Not content with the challenge of the paddling in these conditions, Jaquie put out the fishing line and caught a salmon off the next point. As she was hauling it in, I deployed my towline to keep her from drifting onto the rocks. Just at that moment, the fish hit her paddle and fell off the barbless hook. We watched our supper swim away, and moved off round the corner, determined to make as much mileage down Laredo Channel as we could before camping.

Jaquie:

As a child I tramped through the bush behind my father and the dog, carrying my fishing rod and a tin of worms dug from Mother's garden to a stream where we looked for a good clear pool or a riffle where the brookies might lie. Dad had taught me early on to bait my own hook, then toss it into a likely spot where the tiny weight and wiggling worm would drift the concealed hook down to tickle the fancy of a hungry trout. I almost always caught my share, and cleaned my catch along with Dad's while he lit a small fire in a ring of stones, then waited until there were good hot coals before balancing the old grate over the stones. Out would come the blackened cast-iron pan with a lump of butter dabbed in. On to the fire with it, and in would go the succulent little fish. The splattering and crackling, and the aroma of buttery, browning skin caused our mouths to water in anticipation. I don't remember what else we ate – just the freshest of fresh pink trout.

Occasionally, when Rick and I had exhausted our supplies of fresh meat or fish, I found myself sorting out the lures and looking for an opportune spot where my instinct told me I could catch a fish. Points where there was a good current running seemed like good places to troll for coho. Even at our top speed, we couldn't paddle fast enough to move a lure to attract most predatory fish like salmon, so the combination of abundant nutrients for small species and the speed of the current may have been the magic necessary for successful trolling.

Often the weather wasn't cooperative, and it was risky to troll while battling wind or waves. Then I would tuck into a kelpie bay, anchor to the bull kelp near the point, and jig for rockfish. Seldom were we without fresh fish when we needed it. Among the Copper Rockfish, Quillback Rockfish, China Rockfish and others, we least enjoyed eating Kelp Greenling. The body of the Greenling was thin, the flesh was soft and bonier than the boniest rockfish. A meal of Yellowtail Rockfish is very good, with large firm flakes and a delightful flavour. But some of the pleasure of the meal was offset by the scratches and cuts on my hands from cleaning the big-headed, spiny blighters, however hungry I was.

Rain was blowing into our faces in gusts, mist lay over the water, and visibility was poor. We encountered a very old workboat we first thought was abandoned and adrift. We introduced ourselves to the crew of three that appeared when we paddled near. I scrambled out to meet Bill, Kalyn, and Jamie, log salvagers who were in the process of booming the many useable hemlocks thrown up along the shore by the recent storms. During a four-mile ride to the planned camp we swapped stories, got acquainted, and learned a bit about their business.

Harsh climates and hardship must breed a culture of community, sharing whatever you have with others outside your extended family. On a 1995 trip to Baffin Island, I experienced this attitude among the Inuit. In their culture, your home is open to any stranger that comes by, and you share your possessions with anyone in need. This makes sense, because in the old days this sharing was critical to survival, and survival required almost all of your time. This attitude thrived on the North Coast, but it diminished as we moved to more southerly latitudes.

Jaquie:

What a remarkable day! The wind and rain enclosed us in a grey, misty world with little visibility as we ground along against a strong southeast wind and an ebbing tide. I fished awhile against Rick's good sense, but did hook a coho and as I reeled it in, my mouth watered in anticipation of the rich, juicy dinner we would cook.

Then my paddle slipped into the water on the starboard side, and the fish ran toward the boat – right under it, rising and hitting the paddle just as I reached for it. My spirits fell as I watched it flip and swim away. We have some tinned meat and cheese left, but I'm conscious of conserving it for an emergency. The protein and iron in the salmon are so necessary for us, and the fresh fish is awfully satisfying when it is available.

Time seemed to slow, the damp crept into my bones, and my energy fell lower. I tried to estimate how long it would take to reach the farthest visible point, dividing the distance into little do-able chunks to keep my falling spirits from overwhelming me. Rounding one of these markers, I strained to make out a shadowy boat against the sheer rock wall. It appeared to be adrift and derelict, so I left the comfort of the back eddy and headed into the wind across the bay. As we came in line with her, a figure stepped out on the back deck with a mug in hand, calling, "Would you like a cup of tea?"

To our amazement, the vessel was a log salvage boat with enormous power in her engine, but sorely in need of a new wheelhouse. The crew welcomed us alongside, securing Rick's kayak while they all helped me to struggle my way out of my cockpit onto the rusty, rough deck and into the wheelhouse where we were invited to sit on a bunk and handed a steaming mug of tea and a cookie.

Rick was pleased to get a good look at a bit of chart that he was missing. We were headed for a sandy beach in a bay just ahead, so they towed our kayaks in and dropped us on the beach – our arms loaded with a package of frozen chicken breast, a loaf of bread, and some

Chinese liniment for my ribs. The mist swallowed the big boat, and even the steady rhythm of the heavy engine faded to nothing. In the quiet of the rainy bay, I found it difficult to believe we had actually met. Pure coincidence was at work.

I believe that the shy incredulity and the generosity with which we are met all along the way will be my strongest impression of this trip. I aspire to live the rest of my life, no matter where I am, open to people and their stories in every corner I visit. I will attempt to give back a full measure of kindness and attention to the folks I meet along my life's path.

Tucked into our bay, we were safe from the wind and the sea. As we set up camp, we decided to give ourselves an extra rest day, and we took extra care in creating our camp. Our kitchen was quite a civilized affair, with a waist-high bench, hooks for hanging utensils and a flat log to put our 'Brittlestar' seats on. The Brittlestars are a combination self-rescue device and camp seat. On an extended trip, the comfort of sitting with back support is immeasurable. The kayaks rested on the sand next to the tent, and the paddles became poles to raise and support the tarp, creating a dry space to relax while reading or eating. The tent faced the bay, with a view of 180 degrees, thick treed bush behind us, and a wide beach stretched out in either direction in a gentle curve.

Jaquie busied herself in her kitchen, and baked some soft, fudgy brownies to follow the main course – chicken breast, yams, carrots and cabbage. I puttered with equipment to satisfy my concerns about wear and tear on our boats.

Jaquie:

After organizing the camp for comfort and convenience, it was high time for a bath in the sea. We scrubbed and dunked quickly in the chilly water, but it felt so good to be clean. Rick had a fire going, ready to dry bodies, clothes, and gear once the rain stopped.

We sat watching a flock of shorebirds feeding in the seaweed and debris left by the last high tide. As we watched what appeared at first to be random running and pecking, we noticed the birds moved as if choreographed. Run, run, run – stop and peck at the weeds, then turn 30 degrees and run, stop, peck. As if governed by a single unanimous will, they lifted off the beach to wheel and turn, dip, climb and drop, in perfect unison and formation. This flock of Dunlin (Calidris alpina I think) entertained us with a breathtaking aerial ballet to the shush, shush, shush of the waves against a backdrop of a pastel evening sky. They danced and swung together in the fading light until we could barely see them, then disappeared around the point.

It rained solidly all through the night until four-thirty the following afternoon. We kept the fire going strongly to dry enough firewood, but still had time to take a walk along the shore to watch the southerly seas pounding at the cliffs. It was good to have a rest day. We paralleled our boats at the top of the beach, six feet apart, with a log across the two bows and another across the sterns. I stretched the tarp across this squared frame to collect rainwater, replenishing our water supply in very short time. We collected rainwater wherever possible, minimizing use of chemicals for disinfecting. *Happiness is a full twenty-six litres of pure water.*

Supper that night was tamale pie. This dish became a favourite with both of us, tasty with plenty of bulky protein. As on many wilderness journeys, food often dominated the conversation. We were hungry a lot of the time, but in a healthy way. We knew our food intake was sufficient for our needs, but always looked forward to the next meal. As we paddled along, usually by three in the afternoon, conversation would turn to dinner. We'd spend hours discussing the next meal in mouth-watering detail. Before supper was ready we'd hear our stomachs growling in anticipation. At home in the city, I look at my watch to see if it's OK to be hungry. How unhealthy to base my hunger on such a cerebral motivator as the time of day, rather than listening as my body tells me when it needs calories.

On the third day we set off. The forecast was for the wind to veer to the west. The sky was starting to look ragged as the nimbus broke up, and the weather became more settled. Eleven-fifteen saw us on the water, reluctant to leave our beautiful beach, but eager to get back into the rhythm of moving each day. We made eighteen miles, down and out Laredo Channel, and took a wild ride across the exposed Laredo Sound with a following sea. In a heavy following sea, a wave will lift the stern and drive the bow into the trough immediately downwind of it. Most of the time a paddler can rudder the craft to keep it straight. As the seas get bigger, several forces affect the boat. The crest of a wave travels faster than the trough, so the waves will attempt to pitchpole the craft (turn it end over end). The boat is now balanced precariously on only the knife-edged bow and stern sections with the flat belly clear of the water, very unstable. A kayak rarely pitchpoles, but it can slew sideways, rolling upside down into the trough ahead of the wave. To prevent this, a 'high brace' technique is used – flicking the boat hard into the braking wave sideways and thrusting the paddle blade flat into it for support.

We were whooping and yelling as we slid down the long swells, running past the occasional boomer rearing up through the surf like an angry black monster. As you slide down the lee face of a following sea, your boat accelerates rapidly; this has to be felt to be appreciated. There is an opposite reaction as the wave passes beneath your hull and your bow points to the sky.

You grind slowly out over the top, stall, then ride the next roller to speed your boat down into the trough again.

We headed next for the narrow entrance to Meyers Passage, where we expected to camp. This rocky channel is an amazing formation with towering walls in places, and leads to Klemtu by a circuitous route. The narrow passage must have been a surprising find to the early explorers. From the west it runs six nautical miles east, turns in a sharp right angle to run five miles north, then the route turns 180 degrees to the south for the final five miles to the village of Klemtu.

We reached the western entrance to Meyers Passage mid-afternoon, having paddled the ten miles across Laredo Sound. We originally intended to camp near here, having been told by the people on the salvage boat that the sea runs through the Passage at eight knots on the full ebb.

Jaquie's curiosity and intuition took over. She suggested we push up the channel as far as possible. The worst that could happen was being stopped in our tracks or popped back out again. We pulled into the channel against a slight current, and glided along easily, watching the incredibly lush marine growth on the sea floor. Even though we were still moving against the ebb, in the narrowest part of the channel, we found a current no more than one knot rather than the expected eight. Local advice is good, but experience is better! It was a relief to pass so easily through the narrowest part of Meyers and make another three miles towards Tolmie Channel that night.

Jaquie:

We searched the high rocky spots in Meyers Passage for the pictographs we had heard were there. No luck, but the sea life was amazing. Our boats drifted over thousands of little jellyfish, sun stars, sea stars, plumose anemones, and a bright orange tube worm that I should be able to identify after Andy Lamb's underwater identification course, but can't remember. We found the entrance to a long tidal lake running between the channel and the sound, but didn't go in as the tide had turned to ebb and we might have been trapped for a few hours.

Jody of the La Niña Expedition had advised us of a small shingle beach on the east side of the channel and sure enough, it appeared as if we really knew where it was. The beach was just right for the boats and tent, and we gathered some firewood before settling to make a meal. The riser for the oven turns our pot into a steamer, good for reheating foil packages of leftovers. The remains of the tamale pie with a freshly caught rockfish and cabbage salad made a welcome supper for two hungry, tired people.

The following day, July 5th, dawned calm and grey. After an oatmeal breakfast we moved north, around the corner into Tolmie and Finlayson Channels, and headed south for Klemtu. The strong flood running north past Boat Bluff Lighthouse gave us a good workout. We alternated running the fast eddies, then giving it all we had to make it round the points. We were determined to make Klemtu that night. Could it have had something to do with the thought of a hot shower, a burger at the band café, maybe the laundry, or even the phone call home?

Floating in a kelp bed in a back eddy, we found a basketball reminiscent of 'Wilson', the ball that became a companion for Tom Hanks in the movie *Castaway*. We assumed it had escaped from a lively game downtown. Half a mile from Klemtu, Clarence, a friendly local fellow pulled up in his boat and chatted for a while, welcoming us to the community. We had now passed our 'second century' – two hundred miles and feeling very fit and lean. Klemtu appeared through the rain, and a friendly porpoise escorted us in to the main dock. On our twentieth day out, we looked forward to all that this small village had to offer.

Jaquie and Rick catching the ferry to Pr. Rupert

Ready to pack gear on Somerville Isl.

Full load of food and gear

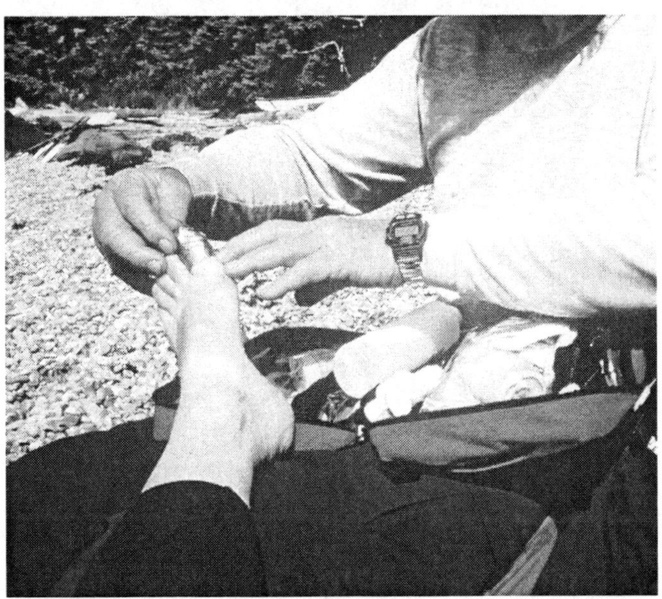

Foot care

Basalt columns in Principe Channel

Salt-rimed rocks and trees

LSD (Log Sort Division) in the mist

Crew of LSD provides hospitality and a chicken dinner

Light house at Bella Bella

Sea lions

Sara on the Beach at Burnett Bay

Rick enjoys a sunset with hot chocolate

Civilized moorage at Shearwater

A humpback whale breaches off the bow of Jaquie's kayak

Starting a cedar basket

A sunstar envelopes the tiny crab trap

Triquet Island reflections

Sara and Mike head home

Rough landing

View N East from Thormanby Ils.

Susumu and his kayak

Rick and Jaquie at Ambleside – Aug. 19, 2001

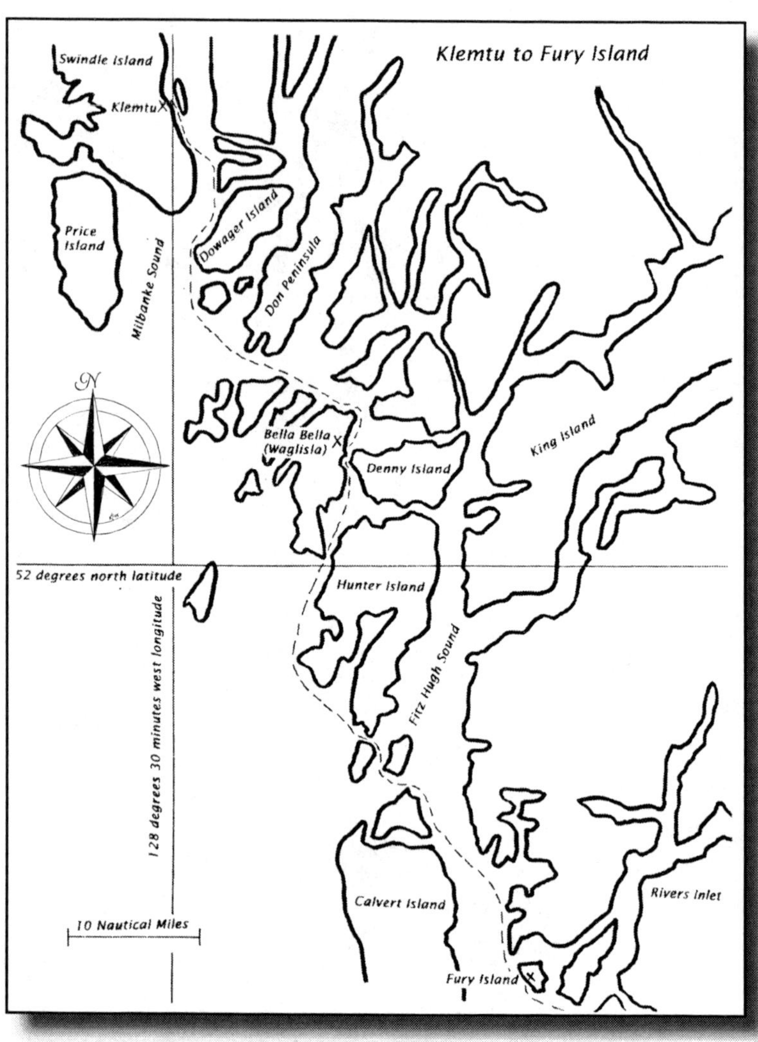
Klemtu to Fury Island
Swindle Island
Klemtu
Price Island
Milbanke Sound
Dowager Island
Don Peninsula
Bella Bella (Waglisla)
Denny Island
King Island
52 degrees north latitude
Hunter Island
128 degrees 30 minutes west longitude
Fitz Hugh Sound
Calvert Island
Rivers Inlet
10 Nautical Miles
Fury Island

Nature's Rules And Natures Cycles:

Traversing The Mid-Coast

Nature is neither for us nor against us. It just is, and it doesn't care. In our superstitious minds, we tend to romanticize the 'Cruel Sea' or the 'Killer Mountain.' If there is a maker, then he or she must be chuckling at our pathetic efforts to attribute human emotion to this totally neutral phenomenon.

The rain persisted, driven by the southerly wind as we tied up at the public dock in Klemtu at two-thirty in the afternoon. Glad to be off the water, we climbed stiffly out of our boats. After our workout against the current in Finlayson Channel, stretching was a welcome relief. Over the last week, my hamburger fantasy had attained epidemic proportions and my lust was satiated at the small restaurant. I devoured a burger with mushrooms, bacon and fries while we chatted with the locals.

We used the laundry and shower at the tourism office and made enquiries about a campsite. The tourism people told us that we could put up our tent on the public dock, but this wasn't too appealing, especially as the dock was covered in tar and creosote. Then we met Evan Loveless, tourism organizer for Klemtu, who arranged for us to stay in a float home a few hundred yards along the shore. Jaquie walked around the waterfront to it while I paddled over, towing her kayak up to the float. We hauled up on the deck, unloaded our equipment, and gratefully installed ourselves in the warmth and shelter of the float home.

Our stay in Klemtu extended to two days while we watched the whitecaps, driven by the southerly storm funneling up the channel between Cone Island and Swindel Islands. During this time we took the opportunity to repair equipment, bake bannock, and explore the settlement. The people of Klemtu were friendly and helpful, and we began to feel quite at home. Unable to find any fresh fish in the band store, we walked over to the small private store at the other end of town but had no luck there either. Jaquie asked a quiet woman who was also shopping if she could tell us where we might get some fish. She said, "Come home with me."

We followed her home in the rain, and waited while she took a package of fresh red snapper from her own freezer for us. Generously, she also offered three tins of salmon she had canned just that morning. Of course we were delighted, and although we offered to pay for them, she seemed a little surprised and perhaps offended that we had tried. We wished we had some jars of our own fresh honey to trade, but bringing much of it from home would have been impossible.

Jaquie has an interest in hand-woven baskets. There was a display of cedar baskets that had been woven in Klemtu by

Violet Neasloss, one of the elders. When Jaquie asked if she could meet her, everyone pointed out the house around the bay where she lived. The woman who gave us the fish directed Jaquie to Violet's house, which was just next door. Timidly, Jaquie knocked on the door and was invited inside to have a visit while I walked along the boardwalk back to 'our house' to catch up on some navigation notes.

Jaquie:

A tiny woman in an apron answered the door when I tapped. A rush of moist, warm air greeted me along with her shy smile as I explained about the baskets and how dearly I would like to ask her about the cedar bark, the dyes, and techniques that mark the coastal artistry. Violet apologized for the steamy house, explaining that she was canning salmon her son had caught for her. She explained that because she has been widowed for a number of years, she depends on family and friends to provide her with the fish and other things from the wild which she prefers over items from the store.

She pointed out her children, grandchildren, nieces and nephews in photos all around the room. She told me stories about them, and pride shone from her sparkling dark eyes as we looked at one photo after the other. Sadness lurked there too, when she spoke of the ones who had been lost to the sea or to diabetes or alcohol in the little community. She shares the grief of many elders in villages all along the coast who lose their young people to the cities, or to jobs on fish farms, or to logging many miles away. My heart felt heavy as I contemplated the sorrow an elder must feel when she sees her community losing centuries of values and skills, when the next generation has no hope or drive to regain the pride and vigour of the old ways. Must changing times extract such a desperate price from a people so recently connected to the land and sea?

We looked at baskets she was working on – many sizes and shapes. The old dyes once used are difficult for her to access, as the people don't visit the old gathering places much anymore. The trade in materials and goods among peoples from other places just doesn't occur as it did. Lately, Violet has been using commercial dyes she orders from the city. She is eager to teach some of the younger women the old patterns and techniques, but is afraid there isn't much interest in these old skills. She worries, will the gifts be lost with her?

She explained how, when her mother was young, the women travelled to special areas to harvest bark from specific cedars without harming the trees. They performed a ceremony to honour the tree and thank it for the gifts it gave the people. She told me the best time of year to strip the bark, how to use the cedar roots, and a host of other tips about native bush lore.

I was sorry to leave the cozy little home and the warmth of Violet's welcome, but darkness was creeping into the bay outside the steamy windows. I negotiated the purchase of a soft, rectangularbasket. It had a pattern that reminded me of one my grandmother kept a collection of spare buttons in when I was a child.

The basket travelled four hundred miles to Vancouver in my kayak, carefully packed and used as a receptacle for eggs and other delicate things we collected along the way. I resolved that, during the trip, I would have to find just the right cedar tree, thank it for the gift of bark, and try my hand at weaving.

Our stay in Klemtu came to be two of the most social days on the trip. Evan came to visit us for tea in the evening and to enjoy Jaquie's fresh baking. The three of us swapped endless stories about our mountaineering exploits. Jaquie's experiences in the Coast Range and on Mt. Waddington, mine in New Zealand and other places in the world, and Evan's in the Rockies and on the coast. By the time we left on the third day we were really feeling part of the community.

Jaquie:

Many years ago I visited a friend who lived in a float home on the South Arm of the Fraser River. That night in Ladner, as I drifted off to sleep, I marvelled at the lightly rocking motion that occurred whenever a fishing boat passed, or a tug towed something by. That rocking feeling was one of the most comfortable and comforting I can remember.

Now I was living in a float home! Even our short stay here will remain in my memory as a magical home away from home. In order to repay the generosity and hospitality of our host, we did a major houseclean prior to our departure.

The floors got a good wash, the bath and kitchen were scoured, and all the rooms vacuumed and tidied. There was a party of kayakers arriving the evening of our departure, and as our way of saying thanks, we wanted to leave this cozy home spic and span.

To catch the start of the southerly ebb we put in at three-thirty in the afternoon of July 7th. As we paddled down Finlayson Channel in the steady rain, Klemtu and our float home receded steadily behind us. Fond memories of Klemtu and the people we met remained, but it felt great to be moving south, eating up latitudes again.

The coastline south of Klemtu has very few landings. We'd

hoped to find a camp by five o'clock, but had no luck. The seas were whipped up now, with their crests breaking over our bows as we plugged steadily south, hugging the shore, taking advantage of any small indentation to relieve the strenuous workout into wind. The ebb against the gale caused a 'wind against tide situation'which tended to steepen the waves, but we found the seas manageable in the two hours before the wind moderated.

Our next decision was how best to cross Finlayson Channel. We were on the Inside Passage ferry route that held serious shipping hazards for us. Prince Rupert Traffic on Channel Eleven on our radio gave us a verbal snapshot of the shipping in our vicinity. We knew the positions of the major vessels in the channel and because ships monitor the same channel, they would be aware of our position and vector for crossing. We waited for the Alaska ferry *Malaspina* to pass, as well as a tug and tow before setting a course for the crossing.

Finlayson proved to be lumpy, but still left us with a reasonably wide safety margin. The seas on our starboard bow were easily negotiated, and we hit the east side of the two-mile crossing at Nowish Inlet with no problem. Once again I called Rupert Traffic, stating we were clear of the shipping lanes, and we turned south. Still looking for a camp, we moved down the coast as the evening wore on, facing nothing but a rocky shore devoid of landings.

Tired and getting hungry, we would have accepted any tiny nook to land in, but miles went by and the day was coming to an end. Suddenly Jaquie shouted, "Look at that!"

Half a mile ahead appeared a beautiful shingle beach on the south side of Oscar Channel. Our spirits lifted as we looked forward to a snug camp and a hot meal. We picked up our pace, all was well with the world again, and we shot across the channel in the last of the ebb and pulled up onto the rocky beach. To our disappointment, it was bisected laterally just a few yards back from the shore by a fast river, preventing even the thought of a campsite.

I struggled across the river through the current, then followed it upstream in the faint hope of finding a flat place above high tide. Absolutely nothing in the shape of a tent site was to be found.

The last of the light was fading as we put to sea again at nine-thirty. The tide had turned to flood, so we had both wind and current against us. We had searched unsuccessfully for six miles, but at ten o'clock, as we turned east out of the south side of Oscar Channel, we found 'Camp Desperation'. A narrow surge channel with a bed of two-foot diameter boulders at its head would have to do. At least the boulders were round and storm-worn, not jagged.

We crashed ashore in semi-darkness, jumped out, and waited until the surf lifted our boats. We dragged them a few feet as they lifted in the surge until they were dumped onto the rocks, then waited again for the next lift. Hearing the crack and crunch of overstressed fibreglass was unnerving. To this day I am amazed how a few millimetres of that material can withstand a 200-pound load crushing it onto rocks. Spending the night at sea in the southerly, bobbing about in the swells, and needing to keep each other awake all night wouldn't have been a good alternative. I didn't think I had enough stories in my head to keep us awake for more than a few hours, anchored to kelp, bobbing and weaving. Camp Desperation was definitely the lesser of two evils.

It's amazing how fatigue can affect your judgment. As we reached the high tide line at the head of the steep beach, I secured the boats to a log before dragging them up into the bush. After pulling at a dead weight, I started to think I was right out of energy. Luckily, Jaquie pointed out that I was trying to drag the log. When you're cold, hungry, and terribly tired, you have to carefully think through every move. Making a stupid mistake near a strong tidal rapid could result in a critical situation or a disaster. We collapsed on the log and laughed at the absurdity of it all.

Supper was anything but a formal affair that night: a can of beans mixed with corned beef heated on the stove, a biscuit, and a drink of water. The tent was up in record time, the food bag was hung, and the boats were safe and secure. We hit the hay as soundly as our precious kayaks had hit the rocks. But the camp was very cozy, and we slept the sleep of exhaustion.

Our twenty-third day was as beautiful as the camp search before it had been miserable. I brought Jaquie a coffee in bed as a morning treat, and then we ate our breakfast of toast and honey in the warm sunshine. It was one of those magic mornings, contrasting so vividly with the night before, so we took our time. We launched at one in the afternoon to head for our next night's objective, Ivory Island. The route was sheer pleasure: open coast with boomers, whoops and hollers as we negotiated the surge channels, sunshine sparkling off the waves, lively seas, beautiful beaches and tiny channels to navigate through. Only in a tiny kayak on the open coast have I had that depth of feeling.

Jaquie:

Today has been such a beautiful paddle between tiny islands and through Suzette Bay. We found a tiny sheltered sand and shell beach for our lunch spot. Between Dallas Island and the end of Dowager Island, we spotted a large, brownish jellyfish, dangling its long tentacles in the water. Some of the little islands on the chart have no names, and south of Clam Passage between Lady Douglas and Salal Island, Rick named one 'Jaqueline Island.' His normal practicality sometimes thins, allowing a shy romantic to peep out! Once more, I thank whatever force brought us together.

Later in the day as we neared Bella Bella where Mike and Sara will join us for the next leg I noticed a feeling of nostalgia and some pressure to hold tight to our solitary voyage. Old experiences of discord and unhappy endings crowd my mind, jostling with my common sense. I am aware that my antisocial spirit and the desire for solitude are at crosscurrents with Rick's social nature. Many of his trips have been with groups of people, where I have tended to spend more time alone. The challenges of this trip are not isolated to weather and sea.

Our dinner of pasta with pesto sauce, tuna, and sunflower seeds, topped with a generous sprinkling of Parmesan cheese has elevated my mood to one of hope and optimism. Fruit cocktail and hot chocolate with Grand Marnier furthered my sense of well-being as we snuggled deep into our sleeping bags to read and write tonight.

We picked out the bright white and red of Ivory Island Lighthouse three miles to the south, punched across a heavy westerly swell, then went counterclockwise around the island, looking for a landing. We travelled three quarters of the way around to the north side exploring the shoreline before finding Speckled-Egg Beach. We named it for the dark-flecked granite rocks and boulders that resemble large, grey, birds eggs that comprised the entire beach.

Inside the forest we found an ideal soft place to set up the tent. Clumps of wildflowers (that Jaquie explained were columbine) sheltered from the wind at the edge of the trees. She picked a petal, then showed me how to nip the tiny bulb at the end with my teeth to savour the sweet nectar inside. Perhaps if the morning is sunny we'll see hummingbirds here.

Sometimes I find it hard to believe that twenty-four hours can produce such extremes in conditions. Our lives are certainly dominated by the dictates of nature. We have long since accepted that we must move with nature rather than try to fight against it..

The visibility was less than a hundred yards. We spent the morning baking raisin bannock and cooking pancakes for breakfast, taking the opportunity to have a warm sponge bath while we waited for the fog to lift. By two o'clock the conditions gave us enough visibility to move off Speckled-Egg Beach. Our route wound through half a mile of reefs into Seaforth Channel on a dead calm sea. The crossing to the south side was easy.

Just off Lay Point, Jaquie caught a 'two-mealer.' The salmon raced around the boat, under the boat, around a small rock, and back again. She kept tension on the barbless hook all the while. This involved some fancy paddle work, spinning the kayak and chasing the fish. With supper secured firmly on deck, we turned into our camp at Spratt Point in Kynumpt Harbour, with mist still curling around trees in the distance.

We toured the inlet, which, judging by the ruined dock, had seen logging and farming operations in its day. There were bits of rusty, old machinery and signs of cultivation right round the periphery of the bay. On the west side we found a great camp, but based on the wildlife tracks and berry patches everywhere, we decided this wasn't the place for us. Pity, because it had an excellent supply of dry firewood. We crossed to the point on the far side and set up camp on a dry, grassy knoll. After camp was set up I paddled back across the inlet to gather firewood, lashing the logs together and towing them back to camp. The ride back was a tough workout. Towing heavy, unwieldy logs while paddling an empty kayak is difficult, and the drag on the light boat caused me to wander and weave my way across the bay. Once the fire was going on the rocky spit, and the salmon fillets were crackling in the pan, the mist cleared. We spent a pleasant evening on our beautiful grassy point.

After supper I started out on the food hauling ritual, but the only big tree available was a shaky-looking dead thing. I managed to get the first hook over a branch and hauled away, with my only firm foothold located right below the load. A crunch or two later I was running for shelter as branch, hookline, and food bags rained down on me. Suffering no more than a glancing blow to my back, I returned in almost pitch darkness to hunt for anything ten feet up off the ground that would hold a hook. All that resulted from this effort was a token cache. I'm just glad no bears came our way that night.

During breakfast, porpoises appeared in our quiet bay. The next high-pressure ridge had arrived, and we basked for a while in the warm morning sunlight watching their fishing antics. Packing up a dry tent is a small but significant pleasure on a dry day.

We launched into the flood at mid-morning and cruised easily through narrow passages to Dryad Point Lighthouse. This picturesque lighthouse inspired us to take several photos before travelling around the headland into Bella Bella, where we arrived at two-thirty in the afternoon.

The band store at Bella Bella was a welcome sight. We needed to stock up on things we hadn't been able to find in smaller villages. Accommodations in Bella Bella didn't materialize so we called the nearby town of Shearwater and secured a room for the night. Looking forward to sleeping between clean sheets, we made short work of the two-mile crossing.

Jaquie treated us to steak dinners and beer in the restaurant then to shake it all down, we went for a stroll along the dock. My stomach must have shrunk due to our lean diet. I felt uncomfortably full.

On our walk we met Ben and Pat Carter from Colorado. Their Sabre 42 sloop was tied up at the jetty, and they invited us on board to meet another kayaker. Al was from Ganges on Saltspring Island. He had been kayaking solo up the inlet near Bella Coola when he met up with Pat and Ben who'd given him a ride to Shearwater for a rest. He was readying to leave for home on the Discovery Coast Ferry.

During our conversation, Pat asked if we carried a crab trap. At some point in our planning we had considered packing one, but explained our decision against the extra weight and bulk.

They showed us their tiny crab trap. It was a three-inch cubed basket with little nylon nooses fastened around it. Listening as they described how it worked, I though it was some sort of toy, but nevertheless I listened carefully. Ben described baiting the trap with fish heads and guts, attaching it to a fishing line with a little swivel catch, then dropping it onto a sandy bottom where there was lots of eel grass. He explained that crabs would approach the feast, and then catch their legs in the plastic slip-nooses surrounding the cage. He went on to explain how he or his wife would reel the little trap to the surface and harvest the legal-sized males. They kindly gave us one of their two traps to keep, wishing us good luck with it. Although still a bit skeptical about the effectiveness of this device, we thanked them and told them we looked forward to the first delicious crab feed.

Today was to be the day we would meet up with our travel companions. Fortunately, the high-pressure ridge was still with us. After breakfast we packed and launched off the dock in warm sunshine to paddle the three miles past Old Bella Bella to Waglisla (McLaughlin Bay) and the ferry terminal. The Discovery Coast Ferry arrived an hour late, but we enjoyed the wait in the sunshine, anticipating the arrival of Sara and Mike, who would join us for the next few weeks. Just a week earlier, they had arrived home to Vancouver from an extended trip through the Middle East, Africa, and Europe. It was time for them to switch from cycling to kayaking mode.

In six short days they'd had to retrieve their boats from mothballs, plan and pack food and equipment then drive to Port Hardy for the ferry. They took the culture change in their stride and didn't miss a beat.

We watched anxiously for them to emerge from the ferry onto the ramp, and they watched just as anxiously for us. We had all the charts, so if we hadn't made the rendezvous, it would have been difficult for them to kit themselves out with enough charts to get them to Vancouver.

With big hugs all around, we were a party of four. All of us worked together to carry their bags and portage their two single kayaks around to the float where we were moored. They sorted gear while we relaxed and made a few phone calls home.

As the bags began to disappear into their boats, we paddled back into Bella Bella and loaded up with supplies such as cornmeal, flour, fresh vegetables, and coffee for the next phase of our journey down to the Broughton Archipelago. With our boats moored, floating alongside the dock, packing our kayaks presented a big challenge. Stowing the stores was accomplished by hooking our knees over the dock rail and resting our chests on the deck of the boat while reaching in and ramming items as far as possible into the watertight compartments.

At this stage of the trip we had packing down to a fine art, but we always had to remember to put a line on the very first bag stowed in order to be able to pull the bags back to the hatch opening. If we failed to do this, the food bags would be jammed so tight in the narrow bow or stern that the only way to get the furthest ones out would have been to lift the end of the boat up and shake it. This is strenuous at best, and extremely difficult in deep water, especially alongside a jetty.

As I packed the last of the white gas, one of my fuel bottles split along the seam. This meant we were down to only three fuel containers. We ended up taking the remainder of the fuel in one of the fragile tins we'd bought the fuel in. This was bulky, but we needed every drop we could carry.

On the way back to Waglisla, my fisherwoman announced, "We usually catch salmon around the headlands. I think I'll drop the line in." Just as we rounded the last point before camp she hooked a salmon, but in her scramble to bring it in, it jumped off the hook. We justified the disappointing experience by deciding that it would be wiser to eat some of the fresh vegetables and a tin of something to lighten the load.

After a brief discussion, we pitched our tents along the beach, celebrated our reunion, swapped stories, and shared a bottle of wine with our supper. We took a stroll along the beach, stopping to admire the house posts that Frank Brown was carving for a new bighouse. After our nightly check of the weather forecast, we all slept soundly under a starry mid-coast sky.

With the morning sun sparkling on a blue sea, we set off south down Lama Passage toward the outside of Hunter Island and the Hakai Recreational Area. Our four Nimbus kayaks sliced easily through the calm water until we rounded German Point, and turned into Hunter Channel to be hit on our starboard bow by a strong southwesterly. The crossing to Mouse Island required a lot of concentration and balance, with the occasional brace, even though our boats were restocked with food – heavy, and very stable. We slid down the alley between the row of small islands off the northwest corner of Hunter, lunching at Want Island along the way, and started looking for a camp in the late afternoon.

With the addition of Sara and Mike, the dynamics of the group had changed. Leadership and decision-making between Jaquie and me had tended to fall to one or the other depending on our specialties. She took the lead in deciding where to camp, what to eat, when to fish, and what our speed. I tended to make decisions about navigation, weather, tides, currents, where and when to launch, and where to hang the food. We discussed decisions unless it was an emergency, but in any given situation there was never doubt about which of us would take the lead.

Now there were four experienced wilderness travellers in the party. This complicated the process somewhat. When it came time to decide whether to go or stay, where to camp or stop for lunch, the four of us would raft up and have a discussion. During the first two or three days as a foursome, I simply rolled on with my navigating and took the initiative because I had been doing it for the last month. In addition, I had the only set of charts, so Mike and Sara were largely in the dark and had to pull alongside me to find out where we were. Ever the diplomat, Sara pointed out that I was taking the role of guide, but that this wasn't a guided trip. We discussed it and solved the problem by rotating navigators on a daily basis, so while we were on the water the person with the chart fell naturally into the leadership role.

We pressed on down the west side of Hunter Island, passing some picturesque coastline. After probing into several small inlets, Sara found us a perfect camp perched on a rocky outcrop with plenty of firewood jammed into a surge channel. The grassy tent spaces faced into a beautiful Pacific sunset. We pitched our tents and enjoyed our pasta sitting around the fire as the sun went down into a calm ocean – our first camp of four.

Jaquie:

The day began wonderfully well, and we set out eagerly, paddling in pairs most of the time. My misgivings about lost solitude seemed foolish as Sara and Mike and I chattered and bantered, getting to know one another. I had met Sara once or twice, but had only briefly met Mike, and that had been a year before. Watching how much Rick enjoyed having his friends around him, I began to believe that I had been a foolish hermit.

By noon, Rick seems to have withdrawn, and is a bit short when I ask him about a break before a crossing. We aren't a team so much just now. I feel he is trying to separate and become less my mate. My personal demon taps me on the shoulder, and invites himself in. It has been sunny all day, but I can't let the joy of it take me out of this black mood. I shut down during the course of the afternoon, my heart aching, wanting to hide away.

Not until just before we try to sleep can I attempt to share my sorrow with Rick. He tries, but I don't believe he un-

derstands my powerlessness in this miasma. Tonight I want to go home. I lie awake a long time thinking about how to be a joiner instead of a loner.

Next morning saw us winding our way through the myriad islands of the McNaughton Group in light fog on a calm sea. Visibility wasn't too difficult to navigate in, and the fog finally gave way to a low overcast and heavy swell as we burst out through Cutlass Sound on to the outside coast. We romped through heavy swells around Superstition Point, and ran past Swordfish Bay, admiring the shattered rocks and wind-blasted trees as we headed for Spider Channel. The wind and rain were really driving, and we were getting hungry. I found a small nook out of the wind where we rigged the tarp and cooked soup for lunch. Eating our bannock and soup, the snug shelter of the tarp provoked stories about other journeys and other storms we had shared, both on the water and in the mountains.

The tide crept up, subtly informing us we had to move off our small sandspit – mainly by threatening to float the kayak to which the tarp was anchored. We needed the motivation to move out, and were soon on the water again, pushing down Spider Channel, past the Edna Islands, and into the beautiful beach on the north side of Triquet Island. With the rain persisting but the seas now sheltered, we set up camp and enjoyed focaccia bread by Jaquie, with veggie stew by Rick. Jaquie made an oatmeal and brown sugar crumble called 'Rickety Uncle' and Sara made fried bananas with Grand Marnier and custard to share around for dessert. *To bed with full tummies again!*

Triquet is part of the Breadner Group and lies exposed to the power of the Pacific from the west round to the south. But the campsite on the north side is leeward, and calm in most winds. Many travellers before us have sheltered here, adding small improvements to the campsite such as an iron grate for a fire grill. The camp even boasts an outhouse without the house, but with a superb view overlooking the bay.

Early in the morning I walked to the weather side of the island, climbing through the huge logs thrown high on the shore, which bear testimony to the power of the exposed Pacific. We treated ourselves to a long, lazy pancake breakfast, finally hitting the water at noon. We moved east across Kildidt Sound to the Serpent Group with its inhospitable cliffs and nonexistent landings. As we surfed the following seas on the two-mile crossing from the Serpent Group, we passed two humpback whales and a big bull sea lion. The sea lion passed by only a hundred feet away, going at tremendous speed, wake streaming back from its head. He seemed very focused on his destination, hardly giving us a glance.

Stirling Island, our lunch stop, gave us an opportunity to dry our tents and lie in the sun, soaking up the rays after the intermittent periods of rain. On Stirling Island we thought about our cat, Sterling, and wondered what he was up to and whether he had made friends with our house sitter. (Of course he wasn't thinking about us at all. He had totally forgotten about us and was being loyal to the house sitter who fed him and even let him sleep on her bed at night).

Since arriving home, many people have asked us a perfectly reasonable question: what the weather was like on the trip? The first time I was asked I said I didn't know! After getting those benign, understanding looks usually reserved for seniors, I would explain the reason. On any long trip you pass through so many weather patterns that you get wet, you dry out, you get wet again – and in the end it all averages out to just 'weather.' Not so on a trip of a week, where you can get seven days of rain or seven days of beautiful high-pressure ridge conditions. In such a case the weather is remarkable. In other words, you *remark* on it, and it sticks in your mind as a great trip or a lousy trip for weather. On our long trip we found that a week of rain or a week of sun disappeared into the past and was quickly swallowed up by time. We both can clearly remember the weather conditions at any specific point along the coast, but overall I just say it was average, because that is exactly what it was.

We threaded our way through the small channel between Hunter Island and Stirling Island, then Mike and Jaquie stopped to fish the rock wall near Underhill Island. I paused a hundred yards off shore in the dead calm while the others were pulling in rockfish. It was so peaceful sitting in my kayak that I drifted off to sleep and actually dreamed.

When the others decided they had caught enough fish, we all moved down Edward Channel through the Planet Group (Jupiter, Mars, Mercury Islands) and out across Hakai Passage. This is one of the entrances from the open sea into Fitzhugh Sound and the village of Namu. It can get quite rough in a westerly, but we had a pleasant crossing with virtually no wind and only a slight tidal drift. That night, after rounding Kelpie Point, we camped in Goldstream Harbour, which is very sheltered and has a small shingle beach that can just fit two tents.

That night, a Saturday, over a stubborn fire in the rain, I cooked a pretty basic meal of canned beans, salmon, and dehydrated potato. I don't actually know who was more stubborn, me or the fire, but in the end I won. Actually we would have had supper an hour earlier if I'd had the sense to use the stove, but oh, what a point of pride it is to cook with wet wood! *Thank you for your patience, Jaquie, especially when you haven't eaten for many hours and have been burning calories at a tremendous rate.*

Our thirtieth day turned out to be a memorable experience, as it included a cave grotto, surfing the rollers on our crossing, a humpback whale, and a fast luge on a following sea down to Fifer Bay on Blair Island. We had left Goldstream Camp at noon and were looking for a water source down the west side of Fitz Hugh Sound.

I located a lake outlet on the chart, so we tucked in to the small bay and searched around for the creek. A trickling of water across the muddy foreshore and the sound of rushing water higher in the bush suggested a bushwhack to a natural shower. In order to reach the waterfall I had to wriggle through a three-foot gap under a huge, precariously balanced chock stone the size of a large house. I remember thinking how slim the chances were of this thing shifting. The rock had been there for hundreds of years. This observation was closely followed by the sinking realization that it has to shift *one* day. Nonetheless, I just got on with it, and filled the water bladders. The other three then crawled under the rock to wash the salt out of their hair and off their skin, emerging clean and refreshed but shivering. We moved on, glancing over our shoulders to the chock stone which of course was and probably still is there, awaiting its geological time to move.

Although the direct crossing of Fitz Hugh Sound is only three miles, we sliced across on a southeast diagonal and made the distance of five miles. I had called Prince Rupert Traffic to ascertain that there was nothing fast and aggressive like a cruise ship preparing to cross our bows. Prince Rupert hadn't mentioned it, but we did watch a humpback whale crossing in front of us, steadily making its way north up the shipping lanes. Despite its massive size, it was difficult to see in the heavy swell.

We surfed with the nor'wester on our tail in quick time to the mainland. After a shortlanding for lunch, we followed down through Fairmile Passage and ran past the Corvette Islands. A huge following sea chased us, and amid wild hoots and hollers, we surfed around into the calm behind Addenbroke Island. I managed to snap off a couple of shots of Jaquie with the front half of her boat in the air as she shot forward off the dramatic seas. We set up camp on Blair Island in Fifer Bay for the night. By hauling rocks at Fifer Bay we were able to clear a campsite and slept soundly in the silence of the sheltered cove.

Jaquie:

What a wild and woolly day! The wind came out of the northwest producing big waves to surf on, and the sun shone each time we pulled out for a break. Mike spied humpback whales on our long diagonal crossing of Fitz Hugh Channel and pointed them out as they breached in the heavy seas. Our camp spot was also occupied by a float, and a log salvage boat with a crew of three. We didn't like to intrude on their side of the spit but just before dusk, one of the fellows motored over in his dinghy to invite us to camp on their float. We declined out of a desire for privacy and space. As we have often done since Mike and Sara have joined us, we shared dessert – tinned peaches and Sara's freshly baked chocolate brownies, were enjoyed along with a special treat. Mike has invented a deliciously sinful after dinner potion of Amaretto and orange liqueur that they have named 'Magic.' Apparently, 'Magic' has raised their spirits on many a cold and inhospitable night in the outdoors. As we all prepared for bed we heard strange swimming sounds in the darkened bay behind us, but have yet to determine the origin of the sounds. Perhaps the sounds were related to our imbibing in 'Magic'.

After our breakfast of granola and fruit, Jaquie baked a muffin loaf while we packed and loaded. We wandered around the point to visit our neighbours and met the crew of the log salvage boat. We sat in our kayaks in the warm sun, and chatted to John and Kelly while we watched Kelly fillet the salmon he'd caught early in the morning. Mike traded a loaf of his freshly baked bread for one of the large coho, and we nibbled on scrap bits of the raw salmon while Kelly worked.

They gave us some tips on fishing with a hoochie and suggested we use a bit more weight than we were using. We loaded our trolling line with two carabiners to give it more weight and depth. Voila! As she trolled down Fitz Hugh Channel, Jaquie caught another coho. We filleted it at lunchtime at a beautiful 'tropical' beach.

Jaquie:

What a paradise I found myself in today! We pulled in to a perfect little beach, an old decaying shack evidence of another's delight here. The water flowed over warm, white sand and after I had cleaned the fish at the far end of the beach, I stripped off to wash and swim in the sand-warmed, blue-green water.

We lolled on the shore eating lunch and dozing until we gradually pulled ourselves up and into our kayaks. The Universe is kind and gentle with me. Rick is kind and gentle with me, too.

Two easy hours further on found us at Fury Island beach. As we drew close to this fabulous white sand haven, we saw a couple sitting comfortably on a log. Our hearts sank at the thought of missing out on a tremendous-looking campsite, but our worries were unfounded. Gibby and Terry, from the converted packer the *Sea Mark*, were cooking wieners on a stick and invited us to share the fire. *Sea Mark* was anchored behind Fury Island, and we spent the afternoon with them until they eventually rowed their dinghy back to their boat, leaving us with an open invitation to drop by for a 'snort.'

Up went our tents, and then Jaquie took the crab trap out to find us a crab. But we were skunked. Sea urchins seem to move with unbelievable speed when fish heads are the bait! We have yet to catch a single crab. Perhaps my initial skepticism at the design is warranted after all.

We indulged ourselves that night with salmon, accompanied by rice, cabbage and carrot salad, white wine, and rice pudding with coffee for dessert. Another evening of indulgence, but as we have reached the three-hundred-mile point, we felt justified. Jaquie and I are halfway through our journey. *Life's good, and we're feeling fit and lean.*

Fury Island was so ideal that we were reluctant to leave. As we had only taken three rest days in thirty-two, we decided to stay a second night. As we lay on the sand enjoying one of those long, slow pancake mornings with endless coffee, two pods of Orcas cruised by. We paddled lazily across the bay to a fresh water creek for water and a good bath. It seemed only neighbourly to drop by the *Sea Mark* for a visit with Gibby and Terry. They took much delight in showing us around their summer home.

The *Sea Mark* has been converted into a very comfortable but shipshape home, with many comforts and contrivances added over their summers of cruising on the West Coast.

Late in the afternoon we tumbled down the hatch to our boats, armed with two little fresh loaves of bread Terry had just taken out of the oven. A quick supper of soup and fresh bread with cheese became a feast with dessert. Mike's cookies – peanut butter with white chocolate chunks – *oh boy!* We two retired to our tent with big mugs of hot chocolate laced with Grand Marnier. To this bliss, were added dreams of trips past and many more to come.

One of the challenges in kayaking is riding very low in the water. Our horizon is realistically only two miles away. We can't see beaches or surf to define coastlines on a crossing. The far side of the crossing looks like a grey hedge, and islands or headlands merge into the backdrop of the far shore.

The chance of hitting a target on a crossing with poor visibility, when following a compass bearing, is very remote. We solve this problem by offsetting the compass course well to the left or right of the target. When we reach the other side, we know on which side of the target we have arrived. We now simply follow the coastline in the appropriate direction to find the place we want to reach.

Binoculars are a great help in situations like this, but I had never much bothered to carry them. Sally bought me a pair some years back and since then I found them very useful on kayak trips. I brought them along on this trip, but due to the accelerated wear and constant exposure to the weather, one of the lenses had fogged and then somehow twisted inside the barrel. After half an hour with a file they became a monocular. My monocular served me well for the remainder of the trip, and was easier to stow in my lifejacket to boot!

Jaquie:

Camps have grandeur or grunge, are light or level or wet or rocky, but no two have been the same. We often muse about the centuries before our passage and imagine dugout canoes pulled up on the long open beaches with cooking and smoking fires announcing to all who pass that The People are busy and prosperous. We have stood quietly in a clearing before enormous house posts holding ancient beams over the descending levels of an arena or theatre, while the moss yields up drips of rainbow-coloured rain. The light in the trees has a glorious quality of gold and green, and the silence of these sacred spaces enters your bones with a palpable weight. I say a prayer of thanks and goodwill to the Ancient Ones who have permitted us this peep into a long ago life.

A camp at the site of an old farm north of Bella Bella gave us an opportunity to examine rusting machinery in a tangle of wild roses. The heavenly fragrance was carried to us amid the swelling sound of bumblebees in the blossoms.

I watched as Rick towed a raft of uncooperative and cumbersome firewood across the bay to our rocky camp spot, his wake wig-wagging across the still water. Having a dry tent and going to bed with dry feet is such a primal delight!

Protected bays with muddy bottoms are the least lovely launch sites. One struggles to stay upright while carrying heavy loads of gear through deep, sucking mud.

It clutches and tears at sandals, it slimes and clings to skin and clothing. The deadly stuff coats the bottom of boots and we skid on rocks as if on grease. The smell of this mud on our gear as the sun warms it is one of rot and decay, and the fecal matter of nameless creatures of the dark water.

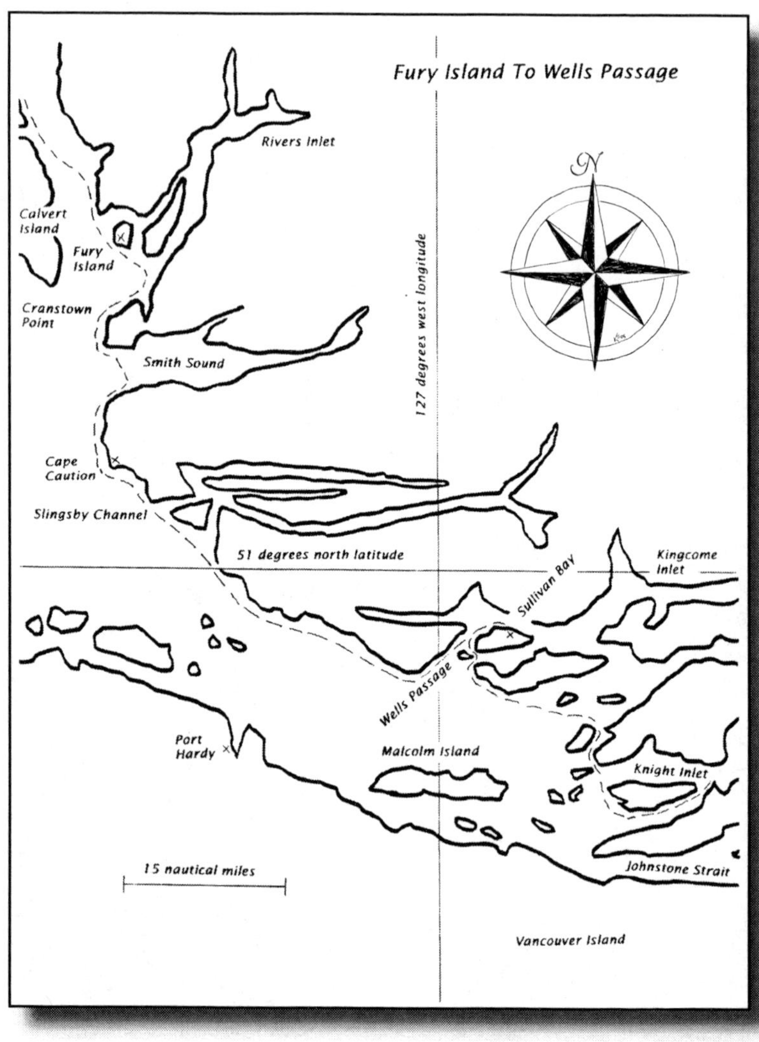
Fury Island To Wells Passage
Rivers Inlet
N
Calvert Island
Fury Island
Cranstown Point
127 degrees west longitude
Smith Sound
Cape Caution
Slingsby Channel
51 degrees north latitude
Kingcome Inlet
Sullivan Bay
Wells Passage
Port Hardy
Malcolm Island
Knight Inlet
15 nautical miles
Johnstone Strait
Vancouver Island

Rivers Inlet:

And Beyond

If our fear is of the unknown, perhaps a dimension of that is fear of the future. The past is unchangeable, gone. In present crisis it's unlikely we feel fear in the moment. Endorphins and adrenaline are in overdrive and our mental and physical focus is towards a solution. The fear and the shakes only set in afterwards.

Considering fear in my life, I get a vision of myself and climbing partner Stephen Fowler outrunning a huge ice avalanche below the Gun Barrel, a glacial chute on Mt. Cook in New Zealand. We'd attempted the summit, but were retreating from 11,000 feet due to the extreme cold.

At about 8 am we were descending the Linda Glacier between Mt. Cook and Mt. Tasman. A third of the glacier broke off Silberhorn above us on the shoulder of Mt. Tasman. At the crack and thunder, I looked up to see a mass of ice cascading slowly toward us down fifteen hundred feet of vertical rock. Ice filled the throat of the canyon directly above us, most of it exploding downwards in our direction. A secondary wave of ice blocks shot back uphill towards the Gun Barrel as it responded to the overwhelming hydraulic pressure in the gut. Then, I remember hundreds of tiny ice shards travelling at fantastic speed out of the blue sky, needling my face as the outrunners hit us.

Roped together, Stephen and I leaped across crevasses, running for our lives in the deep snow, even though we were loaded down with crampons, harnesses, packs, ice axes, and helmets. I had my ice axe in my right hand and my camera strapped to my left wrist as I had been taking a shot of a huge crevasse we'd crossed on a snow bridge. I flipped the camera into my hand and snapped off a shot. I remember thinking this would be the scoop of the year when they found me and developed the film. I even had time to work out how deep the rescuers would need to be probing. At that moment we were hit by a lung-expanding wave of compressed air, then plunged into total whiteout as the pulverized ice formed a dense fog all around and over us.

The ice-fog cleared quickly. We were awe-struck at the sight of a massive tongue of ice rolling down on us. I thought we weren't going to make it, and wondered what death would feel like. Would it be a sudden 'lights out?' Would we be rolled and pounded for a few seconds, conscious of the battering our fragile bodies would take?

Due to my endorphin-enhanced state of awareness, I felt as if time passed with a detached slowness. In fact we had run a hundred metres in snow in about eighteen sec-

onds and the 'slow moving' ice had actually fallen, then hurtled a half mile further in thirty seconds. Only lying on the snow, looking back at our tracks emerging from under a pile of ice blocks the size of five-ton trucks, did the shakes set in. My heart felt as though it would jump out of my chest from the sheer exertion of our desperate sprint. In aftershock, we recovered our breath and chattered and laughed insanely about what would have happened had we run in opposite directions roped together. We agreed it would have looked like a mad Monty Python skit to anyone watching. I believe someone up there looked after us that day because in the tiny tick of time it took to fill the huge crevasse, we made our escape. If we had been on the upper lip, Stephen and I would probably still be there, inside the Hochstetter Icefall, creeping our hundred-year journey down and into the Tasman Glacier, still roped together.

Cape Caution has a sobering name. We looked upon Cape Caution as one of our potential challenges, but what if it had been called Cape Benign, or Cape Calm? Would our vigilance have been any less? I don't think so, but our anxiety factor definitely would have been. Rational fear is an extremely useful tool for tempering our judgment. It's the great sobering influence on the endorphin-testosterone-adrenaline cocktail. I would be very wary of approaching any hazardous situation partnered with someone who has no fear.

We were winding our way through the dozens of small islands and tiny passages that border the northern approaches to Rivers Inlet. Eagles, seals, martens, ravens, and salmon were abundant through this traverse. We reached Rivers Inlet at the high slack. Just north of Bull Island I spotted a Coast Guard vessel approaching and called it on the radio. I wondered whether they could see us on radar, because without a radar reflector on a kayak, I am aware that BC ferries cannot pick us up, even at very close range. I gave the officer of the watch our relative bearing off his bow and asked him to call me when he had us on his screen. They had closed to one mile before they could pick us up.

Thanking him, we continued on past Bull Island and into Duncanby Landing. This fishing resort and marina is built on pilings up against the rock, clinging like a sea star, all weathered wood and smelling of diesel. Down the inlet we could see the crumbling remains of a fishing cannery, active in the early part of the 20th century, long before today's huge factory ships that process fish offshore.

It was laundry day for Sara and Mike, and time for a burger and a beer for Jaquie and me. While we relaxed in the little restaurant, a large humpback whale surfaced and blew close to the dock. It gave us a surprise to see this huge creature so close in the little bay and we scuttled out on the deck to stare, sharing binoculars produced by the staff. The locals showed no surprise and told us the whale often came in and that it had been around for a day or two, just cruising about and feeding. After our rest, meal, and clean up, we left Duncanby on the six-mile leg to Cranstown Point. This turned out to be an all-out slog against the westerly wind and we were glad to pull up on a half-mile beach on the wafer-thin neck of the peninsula.

As we drew near we saw a curl of smoke, a white kayak and one tent at the back of the beach. We landed a respectful distance away, then walked over to introduce ourselves to the occupant. The friendly man's name was Susumu. He told us how he had arrived in Vancouver from Japan a few weeks earlier. He explained that on Vancouver's Granville Island he built a wood-framed Baidarka, an Aleutian kayak, then set off alone for Anchorage, Alaska.

That evening Susumu and I spent four hours over our charts, trading campsite information. He showed me all the camps to the south and I gave him the ones to the north. We spent a good evening together and in the morning, we bade him farewell on his long journey north.

After he left we discussed what a difficult job he must have launching in the mornings. He cannot drag his kayak as we can, because although the ballistic nylon sheath on his boat is incredibly tough, when it's heavily loaded it can get sliced on an oyster or barnacle. This means he has to place his vessel at exactly the right point on the beach so that when he has loaded all his equipment, the tide will come in and lift his boat. With a twenty-two foot tide range on the North Coast and different slope angles on the beaches, this takes a lot of experience. If you're too far down on a flood tide, the boat can get away from you before you've loaded. If you're too far up on an ebb, it may leave you stranded for six hours – or you must unpack, move the boat, and repack. Susumu obviously had launching down to a fine art, because the moment he had finished loading, his Baidarka gently lifted off, and he was gone.

That night on Cranstown Beach we had the option of a camp up in the bush, but since we like to sleep in the open where possible, we decided to camp on the beach. After some highly scientific calculations, we worked out how high the high tide would rise. We laboured with paddles held vertically at the present tide limit, took levels from the tent site, and calculated times at great length. At most locations there are two high tides and two low tides each day. However, the two highs are at different levels as are the two lows. Our results put the higher of the two high tides six inches in front of our tent at ten minutes before midnight.

It's amazing how sure we could be with our calculations, yet how much we doubted ourselves when we were snug in our sleeping bags watching the water lapping almost at the vestibule of the tent. I finally weakened and scrambled out just before the tide was due to peak. Convinced we were about to be flooded out, I hauled a log in front of the tent, dammed the log by shovelling a hasty sandbank, and stayed up to watch. Our calculations were dead on. The tide receded after midnight without even attempting to wash away our emergency dam. What a waste of time and sleep.

So as Susumu moved north towards Anchorage, we moved south towards Vancouver. I wondered if we would ever meet again. The wilderness travel community is an amazingly close network, and I find I have closer bond with, say my friend Dieter in Munich who I met on Kilimanjaro, than with a neighbour I see nearly every day. So I think its quite likely that I'll see Susumu again.

That morning, on the smooth sand, we had the luxury of an easy launch and pushed on down the coast towards Smith Sound. An exciting burst through a wild surge channel on our way out to the open ocean set the tone for the day, and then we were out with the whales. Kelp Head projects well out into the Pacific, but gave us no trouble as we slid down the big swells, in ecstasy with the freedom and exhilaration of the outside coast. We stopped briefly, catching some rockfish and a kelp greenling for our supper. Then it was on to the northwest fast train again, and the following seas soon pushed us through the notch between Tie Island and Extended Point. In no time we were rocking across Smith Sound, taking a direct three-mile line from Shield to Chest Islands. There were whales, whales, and more whales. Tail flukes, water vapour plumes, and shiny backs glistening in the sunshine added to the excitement of the day.

One of our anticipated challenges was boredom. Before the trip we wondered what would happen if we got just plain dejected with every day following the same old routine. Suppose we started to ask ourselves what had possessed us to embark on such a trip? What could the point be of such a long trip? But the reality couldn't have been more different. Every day presented stimulating differences: scenery, wildlife, the physical challenges and weather. Certainly there was the daily grind of the carry. This had to be done twice a day, every day, regardless of all other events except when we were stormed in. Even the carries were different. Our strategy varied depending on the steepness of the beach, the rock obstacles, the landing place, and the state of the tides. Throughout our journey, boredom didn't have a chance to even enter our consciousness.

On mountaineering trips when pinned down by a storm for a week or more, you really need a good tent partner – one who is compatible, willing to indulge in long conversations, or who doesn't mind long periods of silence. The stresses of being tent-bound under such conditions are perhaps even higher than the actual climbing.

Our journey was different. The numbers of stormbound days are fewer on the water than in the mountains and we could always climb out of the tent to stretch our legs or move around without risk of getting blown away. And unless kayaking in the high Arctic, there is less chance of being frozen outside the tent on a beach than on a mountain. Many mountaineering friends have taken up ocean kayaking as an alternative wilderness travel because their knees are worn out. I suspect in many cases it's the pleasure of the easy life that's the attraction. How else can we travel in safety, moving three hundred pounds of weight by our own efforts, go to bed clean every night, and carry luxuries such as canned food, good wine, and a board game?

With our Smith Sound crossing behind us, we pulled into Jones Cove for a late lunch then followed the coast around Milthorp Point, gradually turning to the south. Cape Caution was now only five miles ahead. We needed to position ourselves with the best possible advantage for a burst past the cape in case we were threatened by a low-pressure system. The swells were quite heavy as we began searching for a good landing and camp. Mike and I pushed into a wide surge channel, passed a seal with a big salmon in its mouth and entered a beautifully secluded crescent beach. Without discussion we instantly agreed this was the ideal place. Jaquie and Sara were just little dots, whale watching out in the open ocean. Mike located the tent sites while I barreled back out through the surge to beckon the women in to the shelter of the snug little cove.

We pan-fried the greenling whole, and it went down with rice and peas for supper, enhanced by Sara's spicy fish soup. We all agreed that the rockfish are nicer, so in future the greenlings will escape the hook to swim another day. A starry sky covered us like a shattered blue glass canopy as we dozed off to the familiar sound of the crashing surf. The hazards of Cape

Caution and Slingsby Channel exist, but tonight there is only this magic Pacific night stretching forever over our heads.

We were pleased with a forecast for the continuation of the high-pressure ridge. We woke up to radiation fog, a common occurrence at this time of year, and a sure sign of a fine day. By noon the fog had disappeared so we loaded, put in, and crossed the wide sweep of Blunden Bay approaching Cape Caution. All seemed to be going well so far, but some concern and perhaps anxiety showed in our faces as we neared what we felt could be a critical point on this section of coast.

The waves became compressed, pounding with heavy hydraulic pressure against the rocks of the headland. When they cleared the obstruction, they seemed to feel the freedom of the open sea beyond, lengthening their stride. The northwest wind held the seas on our tail as we surfed past the cape, sliding down the long waves, ruddering for stability, and racing downhill into the southeast. Our speed increased with the wind as we raced past Silvester Bay, rounded Raynor Point, and moved into picturesque Burnett Bay. Jokes and whoops indicated our relief and delight at the release of tension that had built up from the various stories of bad weather and bad luck related by mariners. Perhaps we also felt a little anticlimax at the lack of difficulty. We'd only made five miles, but Cape Caution was now behind us.

Passing a feeding whale, we gently 'shooshed' onto glistening wet sand at the north end of a two-mile long beach. An easy landing here is a great treat. Burnett Bay regularly experiences heavy surf, and kayak landings can be difficult. The challenges ahead are the tidal rapids. Vancouver Island squeezes the incoming and outgoing tides against the mainland and strains the seas through hundreds of channels and islands.

The long carry up the beach was worth it for this superb camp. Burnett Bay is stunningly beautiful, exposed to the southwest, offering spectacular sunsets. Our pasta, salmon, and cabbage disappeared quickly, then we carefully calculated our crossing of Slingsby Channel, our objective for the next day. Slingsby empties one of the most constricted tidal rapids on the coast. Inland from the coast, there is a huge sea, covering many square miles of inlets and channels. The enormous volume of water in this system must exit and access through this one channel four times a day. The narrowest point of the rapid is at Tremble Rock in the Nakwakto Rapids, which run at thirteen knots. Several folks we have met along our route have related experiences of rough seas crossing this stretch in their large powerful yachts, and we are determined not to get swept up into Nakwakto or out to sea. Again we must time our departure carefully. The danger is the ebbing current running west, and if combined with a strong westerly wind, the 'wind-against-tide' situation causes huge standing waves.

We treated the area with a great deal of respect. Our strategy was to cross the one-kilometre entrance at slack tide, preferably on a day with no wind and no fog. This can be a tall order for the month of 'Fogust.' We had two windows of opportunity that day. The first opportunity would occur at eleven-thirty, fifteen minutes before Nakwakto turned to flood and started to run inland. The second would be at five o'clock, 30 minutes before it turned to ebb and began its run to the open sea.

We missed the first window when fog rolled in and wouldn't allow us safely off the beach. Normally, fog wouldn't bother us, as we could take a compass bearing on an easy crossing or use the coastline as a handrail. However, we wanted maximum security for this traverse and chose to err on the side of caution. We waited until the afternoon and launched into the surf at three to catch the five o'clock slack at Slingsby. Time passed slowly but we busied ourselves with our gear – packing and repacking, considering our loads with an eye to stability and windage.

Rounding Lascelles Point at the northern entrance to the channel we had everything lashed down securely, wetsuits over warm clothing, paddling jackets on. We felt ready for anything.

To our surprise, Slingsby turned out to be another anti-climax. The sea was glassy calm with no perceptible current. In fact, halfway across we drifted and took photos of seabirds. I remember a distinct feeling of disappointment. All that adrenaline and preparation for nothing! But that was followed immediately by a second thought. This was exactly *why* we had spent all that care doing the calculations. We were right on time, dead on slack, so the crossing gave us no trouble whatsoever, and another obstacle had been overcome.

Our journey continued down the coast past Bramham Island and ever south, but by now the afternoon wind picked up, giving us a rough ride. Around the south side of Bramham we went, then into Skull Cove.

The entrance to Skull Cove is very narrow and marked by an *inukshuk*, a stone cairn made in the shape of a person. The object evoked memories of the previous summer's visit to Tuktoyuktuk in the Western Arctic. *Inukshuks* are a familiar sight to Arctic travellers, but look out of place in the West Coast rain forest. The literal translation from the Inuktituk language means 'like a person.'

We rounded the *inukshuk* at very low tide, just skimming the rocks below. We slipped and slid around in the mud at low tide until we found a wet, gloomy, mosquito-ridden camp in the salal. We affectionately called the spot 'Camp Grunge'. Although we passed several tents and tarps rigged in the trees along the trail, there was no one home at the whale research station located high up on the cliff. Later in the evening, a group of young people arrived and made their way up to the research station so quietly that we slept right through.

My bright spot of the day was time off from camp chores. I read my book and caught up on course plotting while sipping a cup of wine. Jaquie put up the tent and made a soup and salmon sandwich supper. While puttering around camp, she realized she was missing her reading glasses. Retracing the day, she remembered setting them down carefully on a lovely log at Burnett Bay while she'd pulled on a fleece. But there was no point in going back. We still know exactly where they're sitting, glazing blankly and patiently, forever out to sea.

Jaquie:

We kayaked with grey whales all the way from Blunden Bay to Burnett Bay. I will never be able to forget the awe and excitement of being surrounded by these giants feeding all around us, nor will I be able to imagine an ocean without enough food to sustain them. If I can impress upon my family and friends this huge rush of emotion and caring that filled me, and my hope for sustainable oceans, perhaps my grandchildren and great-grandchildren will one day be as moved.

On the northern end of the two-mile beach at Burnett Bay there hides a tiny cabin, not much bigger than a children's playhouse. It was built several years ago by Randy Washburn and has been a haven for many a mariner waiting out a storm. Inside is a tiny wood stove, and dozens of candles perch on every available level surface, ready for the castaway. Two little bunks could accommodate three people fairly comfortably, if we keep in mind that 'comfort' would be relative to the weather. On a stormy night even a tarp in the woods would be comfortable compared to huddling behind a log with nothing but a sou'wester for protection.

The few books we found in the cabin have been well read, and there is a collection of journals containing the stories of many who have passed some measure of time here. Their stories are varied and fascinating, and we all pored over them intently. We read bits aloud to one another, comparing our recent experiences in various places to those recorded by others.

Our little party is experiencing some discord. Sara and Rick have been travelling companions in the mountains and on the water for several years, but it seems they are finding some difficulty with the sharing of navigation. I sense confusion in Rick, and distress in Sara. My nature is to want to fix things, but all I can do is support Rick in understanding the problem so he can work with Sara for resolution. Division in the party at this stage would be difficult and unsafe due to the lack of duplicate charts. This is an excellent opportunity to utilize Rick's team-building curriculum.

Day thirty-seven started with dense fog. As we waited for it to lift, the tide went out. Now our launch was challenged by having to struggle through a long stretch of deep, sucking mud. The mud was the worst I have ever seen, and we sank almost to our knees. It sucked the sandals right off our feet. Digging them back out left us up to our armpits in stinky, sticky black guck. We slid our boats across the putrid surface, partially leaning on them to lighten our bodies and minimize the grip of the mud. As we staggered about, we saw a guided party of kayakers preparing to leave from the small floating dock used by the whale observation team. They wandered about the float, occasionally staring at our antics. We certainly envied them the clean start to their day.

When we had enough water to float our kayaks, we straddled them, cleaning our feet and arms over the side as well as we could before getting into the cockpit. Once afloat we paddled over to introduce ourselves to Crystal, the guide, and discovered she knows Jody Simmons very well. Jody is one of the five women who made up the La Niña expedition that travelled this coast two years previously. Before we'd left Vancouver, Jody had provided us with a great deal of information from her personal journal which had assisted us in the planning of our trip.

As we passed through the narrow gap out of Skull Cove at about nine on one of the lowest tides of the year, we were able to see marine life that's usually totally submerged. We were in awe with the beauty and variety of the underwater flora and fauna, lucky to glimpse something so rarely seen from the surface. As we moved out into the open the warm sun burst through the fog.

We were glad to be free of the gloom in Skull Cove and out in the bright reaches of Queen Charlotte Strait with the sun dispelling the chills and aches in our bodies. Jaquie caught a Spiny Rockfish for our dinner, but soon after snagged the hook and, much to her disgust, lost the weight, hoochie, and hook. Seven miles from Skull Cove we reached Shelter Bay, and decided to spend the night there. It was only lunchtime, but the seductively warm, white sand invited us to sprawl out, soak up the sun, and dry out. It's great when decisions are so easy. The beautiful cove was obviously a popular kayak camp — it had everything, including a kitchen sink!

Sara and Mike retired to their tent early, but Jaquie and I wandered over to the creek for a luxurious fresh-water wash. The cold clear water sluicing over our heads and backs was energizing. Back in camp we took advantage of the evening to do some maintenance on our spare paddles.

The two-part paddles that had slipped together so easily in the shop now jammed when we tried to assemble them. Had we needed them in an emergency, our only option would have been to use them as single-ended paddles, an unsatisfactory solution if we'd been trying to turn a kayak in a twenty-knot wind in a heavy sea. This may seem trivial, but as synthetic material weathers it is exposed to ultraviolet rays and sea salt, and goes through some structural change. We filed away at the ribbed connections, taking off a fractional layer of material until they slid together easily. When the job was done, we were confident we could assemble them quickly and safely if we lost or broke one of our working paddles.

The sun went down in a blaze of orange and the North Island dusk slowly enveloped the mountains to the east. We crept closer to our small fire talking until the last of the embers signalled time to turn in. So far, our journey had taken us thirty-six days, and had brought us 348 nautical miles from the Alaska border. We were enjoying every moment, content to live in the here and now. Our start seemed so far back it was a dimming memory, our arrival home still too far ahead to visualize.

A quiet, benign dawn greeted us, giving no indication of what we would experience later that afternoon. We slipped into the low tide at ten, paddling on a mirror-like calm toward a fish farm on the far side of the inlet. We were curious to see the operation and to meet the staff on the floats as they fed the thousands of small salmon.

With 1.5 million fish, this was one of the largest operations on the West Coast. Our concern about the fish farm controversy occupied much of our conversation for the following days. We were aware that many of the farms we would pass are owned by huge multinational companies, and that they employ very few local people. Many of the fish farms are automated and can be run with only three or four employees on site.

Jaquie:

Paddled past a fish farm and spoke to one of the staff. I am beginning to understand the disillusionment we have heard from some of the Native people regarding fish farming companies – jobs promised in return for leases let by the bands have not materialized. We have seen no Native staff at any of the farms we have passed. A young worker monitoring the feeding cycle described the ferocious winter storms in this exposed channel, and how fish are washed from one pen into another with the waves. There can be no question that fish in the outside pens are washed out into the chuck. Both Rick and I are concerned that the environmental safety of this method of 'containment' doesn't work.

Five miles later we passed another fish farm, then turned into the narrow gut between Robinson Island and the mainland for lunch. The tide rose as we ate, conveniently flooding the gap to let us pass into Blunden Harbour without a portage. Whenever we had lunch in a sheltered inlet on a flood tide, we would tie a bow line to a small rock, using it as an anchor just off the shore. The boats could float free, and it wasn't worth risking damage to the heavy kayaks to drag them over barnacles unless necessary. However, many a kayaker has dozed off in the warm sunshine, only to wake up and see his or her boat anchored offshore in about twenty feet of water, dragged down by the bow. Recovery involves a swim and a dive or a lot of heavy hauling, depending on the size of the anchor-rock. Part of our lunch routine was vigilance by one of the party, and continually shifting the boats to avoid an embarrassing situation.

Another potential danger is losing our boats to the sea while we're onshore looking for a camp. Towards the end of the day we would land several times to examine likely camps. We would haul our boats out just enough to rest bow or stern on the rocks, leaving the rest of the hull afloat. All was well if one of us stayed back to watch the boats, but if we separated or went up the beach together there was a chance the boats could drift away. Of course, one should tie the boat securely at every landing, but practicalities such as the onset of darkness or rising weather often hurried us. But we'd considered this hazard before the trip, and had ensured that we each carried enough equipment on our person to survive ashore without a kayak. Radio, spare battery pack, flashlight, knife, matches, fire starters, prussic line, flares, compass, garbage bags, and food bars were always in the pockets of our life jackets. We were extremely mindful about keeping an eye on our boats, so nothing of this sort happened. Our kayaks were our home, our transport, our suitcases, our pantry, our fresh water supply, and our passport to Vancouver, so we had a vested interest in their welfare.

By the time we finished lunch at Robinson Island, the channel had flooded sufficiently for us to pass into Blunden Harbour. This was a beautiful green paradise along an exposed shore. We explored a bit, noting it was posted Native reserve land with landings prohibited on some parts of the inlet. A nor'wester was gusting quite strongly as we pushed out into the open sea. Whitecaps were building and by the time we moved into the

Raynor Group, the seas were four feet high and breaking on our sterns. I was glad I was sitting in my Nimbus Seafarer rather than in my old Baidarka. The Seafarer has a rudder and a twenty-three inch beam, whereas the Baidarka had no rudder and only a twenty-inch beam. Although I had paddled the old boat for nine years and was quite comfortable in it, a rudder makes life so much easier in a following sea. To a non-kayaker, three inches difference in width at the mid-section doesn't sound like much, but it makes a huge difference in handling and increases the volume of load space enormously. How much nicer it is to be able to carry emergency fuel or an extra luxury snack or two!

Bearing down on the Raynor Islands with twenty-five knots of wind hard on our tails, we were forced to find a landing and a camp as soon as possible. We doubled back and thrashed for all we were worth into the lee of the most westerly island of the group. I tied up against a floating jumble of logs in a small bay, scrambled out of my boat and over the logs. I reached a rock slab, climbed it and – to Jaquie's amusement – began crawling through dense salal looking for a flat place to garden out a camp. No flat spot appeared, so I retreated to my boat, untied it and dropped back into the cockpit.

The wind speed was increasing. Concerned, we made a wild dash with the wind to the central Raynor Island, spied a cove only four hundred metres downwind and surfed full tilt right into it. First in, I thumped up and over a tangle of logs, jumped out and hauled for all I was worth to get my precious boat out of the surf. The logs were driven hard into the cove and choked it from rock wall to rock wall. Mike, Sara, and Jaquie found a slightly easier route into the jam, but it was still a strenuous pull to get the boats to safety.

The weather was brilliantly clear during all of this – normal with a high-pressure system. This made our beached situation more tolerable, and once the boats were secured, we set off through dense brush to find a camp. We found a level spot, and after a couple of hours of hard work, we had cut two snug tent sites and a communal kitchen. The gale was so strong it cut right through the densest bush, so with the cuttings from the tent sites we wove a windbreak for a little relief. The nor'wester blew all through the night. Above our tent two trees rubbed together in the wind, and we lay awake listening to the eerie sounds they made. We heard voices and thought we had visitors, then a baby cried and a dog barked. It was as if the place was haunted.

By morning the wind had increased to forty knots. Progress out of the bay was impossible. We scrambled along the rocks to the point where the seas raged past our little island. Huge blue rollers marched southwards, their breaking crests brilliant white in the morning sunlight. The fury of the seas humbled us as we watched the maelstrom from our safe perch on the headland. For exercise and distraction, Mike used the handy pruners to cut a path across the island. We all trooped through to the south side to get a different perspective, scouting out an alternate launch in case we needed it. But the bay we encountered seemed much the same conditions as the bay near our campsite, so we abandoned the idea of a portage through the bush.

The seas raced past all that day and into the next night. Then at one o'clock in the morning we woke up to… silence. It was uncanny. No wind, no sound of crashing surf, no babies crying, no dogs barking. We were so accustomed to the storm that the quiet woke us up.

We continued southeast heading into the Broughton Archipelago on a bright clear morning. What an amazing contrast to the previous day. Seven miles further down the coast, with Sara in the lead, a big bull sea lion spy-hopped just beside her boat. He was looking at her with brown, liquid eyes that seemed to say, "Look what I can do!" He paralleled us a couple of boat lengths away for forty minutes, all the way to Lewis Cove. From time to time he would show off, rolling over and over and finally catching a big salmon right in front of us. He ate his lunch, apparently enjoying life and his environment, preceding us towards Boyles Point, as if he were a self-appointed fishing guide, then left us to explore the culinary possibilities around the Lewis Islands as we meandered down the coast.

We turned to the northeast, up into Wells Passage, stopping for lunch on a beautiful sandy beach before entering the Broughton Archipelago. Anchoring our boats to rocks against the rising tide, we cooked some soup to go with our bannock. Putting in again, we caught the flood train that carried us along, up Wells Passage at an easy four knots – a real treat as with only a few paddle strokes we were making six knots or better. *Travelling doesn't get any better than this!*

A small choke of islands guards Sullivan Bay, and we slipped between Atkinson and North Broughton Islands before coasting into the marina. Sullivan Bay is a clean, well-maintained and friendly resort anchored to a rocky foreshore. There is little 'dryland' but the floats are lined with floating homes, joined into a grid of 'streets' with delightfully humourous names evocative of the past. Our favourites were 'Coho Cul de Sac' and 'Halibut Heights.'

When we hopped out of the boats onto the main dock in front of the little general store, our initial reception from the owner was cool. Eventually, after a bit of conversation we learned that some kayakers in the past have been less than polite, demanding services and camping areas that are not available, as this marina clearly caters to powerboat cruising. This was a good reminder that we must be ambassadors for our sport. Respecting the fact that this community isn't set up to accommodate our tents, we shopped for supplies then moved half a mile out of 'town' to set up camp on a small island. I cooked a veggie stew, and as we sat around the fire we reflected on the days behind us, and considered the next section of coast and its features.

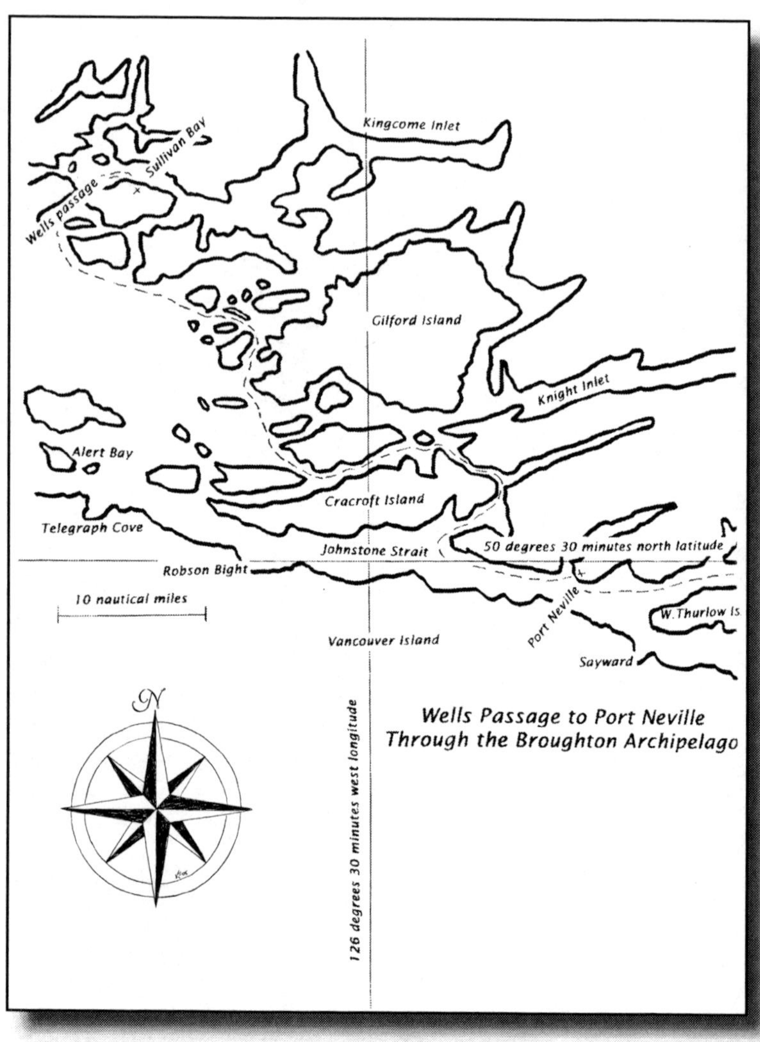
Kingcome Inlet
Sullivan Bay
Wells passage
Gilford Island
Knight Inlet
Alert Bay
Cracroft Island
Telegraph Cove
Johnstone Strait
50 degrees 30 minutes north latitude
Robson Bight
10 nautical miles
Port Neville
W. Thurlow Is.
Vancouver Island
Sayward
N
126 degrees 30 minutes west longitude
Wells Passage to Port Neville
Through the Broughton Archipelago

Winding Through Time:

The Broughton Archipelago

The Broughton route encompasses some of the most beautiful coastline on the planet. Hundreds of islands, big and small, squeeze into the space between Vancouver Island and the mainland of British Columbia. The area has served as a treasure house and home to Native peoples for aeons. This region wears a mantle of timelessness that we sincerely hope endures into the future for all our children's children to cherish.

As I paddled today, thinking about the elasticity of time, I pondered the fact that a sea lion has no e-mail, no voicemail or appointment book, no concept of time or urgency. He just is. This coastal journey of ours seems a huge chunk out of busy lives. But in a few months, time will shrink this adventure to a mere blip in our personal

continuum. There will be no discernible disruption to our income, nor will we suffer from not having to carry out the hundreds of small administrative duties of daily existence at home.

After arriving home from any trip, I am loath to rush into dealing with the umpteen e-mails and voice messages, the pile of letters and little jobs that 'have to' be done. Or do they?

Once when returning from an adventure in Central America, we were sitting at the departure gate in Houston when we heard an announcement. Our flight was overbooked, and the airline offered three hundred dollars compensation to anyone who would take a later flight. Had we taken the offer and arrived home a day later, the calls would have been returned, and the jobs would have been done – just one day later. Our sea lion taught us to work steadily, take time for a little fun, and enjoy the journey. Life's only guarantee is that our lives will run out before our challenges do.

We were running short on fuel for the stove. The water taxi from Port Hardy was due to arrive at Sullivan Bay with supplies the next day. Lynn, owner of the marina, had been kind enough to call on the radio and add four litres of white gas to her order. During our wait, we took full advantage of the luxuries of showers, laundry, and shopping. We even found time to relax in the sun and read, sprawled out on the warm timbers of the float.

Jaquie:

Rick and I have discovered another kayaker here – Steve, from Seattle. He is headed to Alaska and, in the way of most of our small community, inquires about camping opportunities. He and Rick chat a bit, while I putter in the general store. Lynn reveals her relief that our little party lacks the 'attitude' she has experienced with other groups of kayakers. Hmmm. We'll do our best to alert our friends to this when we share our journals back home.

When Jaquie and I returned to camp on the second afternoon, Mike informed us he had evicted a small bear that had wandered into camp. The little fellow had apparently tried using his regular route but had been forced to retreat. We imagined him sitting just out of sight, waiting for an opportunity to retrace his steps, and we promised him we would be gone in the morning. But unfortunately he couldn't wait that long. In the small hours of the morning, I was awakened by the bear tromping past our tent. I huffed my best bear-discouraging huff, warning him we were in the tent. He huffed back and took off at great speed, crashing over the causeway and up the face of the island opposite our camp, disturbing some cranes trying to finish off a good night's sleep on the foreshore. The cranes squawked so loudly they woke up a family of chipmunks, and then the whole forest broke into an uproar. Five minutes later everyone went back to bed and we all slept soundly, though we definitely felt bad about being the cause of the whole episode.

The presence of wildlife was something we expected, parked on a tiny island situated between two larger islands as we were. The whole configuration formed a causeway at low tide, obviously a commuting route for wildlife, but still it provided the only available tent spot.

Apologizing and promising the forest community that it would never happen again, we put in at nine o'clock the following morning in a downpour, perhaps penance for our intrusion. Retracing our route down Wells Channel, we wound our way past Dickson Island on the south side of Broughton Island and along Nowell Channel, heading deeper into the Broughton Archipelago. This took us past Midsummer Island and within striking distance of the village of Mamalilacula. Sea lions abounded on this leg of our journey, and at Screen Island we had to take wide detours to avoid disturbing them on their rocks. Even so, a couple of bulls launched themselves off the top of their rock, striking the water with their characteristic tidal wave on their way out to challenge us.

Jaquie:

What a rainy day! We stopped for our lunch on a slippery, rocky beach. As we huddled over our meal, we were cheered by a school of perhaps eight dolphins feeding. How companionable of them to join us for lunch. Back on the water we saw a whale, tentatively identifying it as a Minke. Then, more dolphins.

In the late afternoon we spotted a rock with some strange-looking golden logs on top. The logs turned out to be Stellar sea lions, who woke up and roared at us as we paddled past. A few did high dives off the top of the rock and swam out to investigate the strange craft. We did our best to maintain a steady pace in case a bull decided to protect his harem. Rick is always conscious of safety and cautioned us to keep our distance, and keep moving. But my delight and curiosity got the better of me. Out came my camera and I captured as many memories as possible before we were out of range.

Mike and I fished for rockfish, and ended up with four of them for dinner. Finding a camp proved a bit difficult. Cold, tired and feeling guilty about breaking a tent pole this morning, I set about unloading both Rick's boat and my own, then prepared a tent site as he repaired the pole. He seemed fairly touchy about having me unload his boat. My reaction was to get ticked off, and I'll admit, I pouted through dinner. I must learn to be willing to confront things like this sooner, even when we have others around. Mike, the conciliator, cleaned all the fish and we fried them up. A pot of rice rounded out a meagre menu, and we went to bed rather more quietly than usual.

That night we pulled into a long, grassy tidal inlet, tired after our nineteen-mile day, but proud of the distance we'd covered. Tomorrow would make it forty-two days out, three hundred and ninety-six miles along our way. Over that night's chicken pot pie, conversation turned to the next leg, where we would be moving through a labyrinth of deep green canyons and tidal passages, vastly different from the rough-and-tumble of the open coast. This part of the journey would require careful computations of current, wind, sea state and timing.

Each of the three route options from this point required a traverse through tidal rapids. Seymour Narrows is the main shipping channel between Vancouver Island and the mainland. The second alternative would be to pass through Okisollo Rapids, out of Hole-in-the-Wall or Surge Narrows into Desolation Sound. The third choice was to traverse Whirlpool, Greene Point, Dent and Yaculta Rapids – that route would spit us out into Calm Channel. We quickly eliminated Seymour due to the shipping traffic and industrial areas near Campbell River. We next eliminated Okisollo and Surge Narrows because they were familiar waters, and we wanted to experience new country. The best choice, after plenty of discussion, seemed to be Whirlpool, Greene Point, Dent and Yaculta. Coincidentally, when traversing them from north to south, they are in ascending order of power, which gives an excellent progressive sequence of experience to boaters in many types of craft. We considered the pros and cons of the routes late into the evening and finally went to bed, looking forward to visiting Mamalilacula the next day.

After our previous long day of paddling, we puttered around camp, treating ourselves to a pancake breakfast and putting in at the fashionable hour of 11 a.m. Soon Knight Inlet appeared round the corner and treated us to a lumpy crossing. We planned to spend some time exploring on Village Island, looked forward to relaxing in the abandoned village of Mamalilacula on the south shore. We looked for a landing on the muddy beach but instead of that, paddled to the west end, where there appeared to be some habitation.

We pulled around the float to the office/home where Tom Sewid, a local Kwakwaka'wakw, lives with his family, and were directed up the trail into the village. Tom was conducting a tour for another small group of people. We joined the group, sprawling out in the sunshine in front of the old longhouse, listening to stories of the past.

Jaquie:

Our charts sometimes reveal a little about the men (presumably) who named the features we pass, but in this area the names reveal little imagination, just a comment on the seasons. We lunched on Midsummer Island as we paddled through Spring Passage. The original peoples of this coast have given beautiful, melodic names to these places. We crossed Knight Inlet to visit Mamalilacula, or Village of the Last Potlatch, on Village Island.

Later, from research on the internet, I would learn that the historian Franz Boas, called the people of this area 'Kwakiutl'. They were the fiercest of all Pacific Northwest Aboriginal groups in the nineteenth century. Their power and territory extended through northern Vancouver Island, the indented mainland shore opposite, and the islands between. We now know them as Kwakwaka'wakw ('nearest to the ocean').

The potlatch, one of the most fundamental cultural traditions of the First Nations of the Northwest Coast, became a clandestine and risky underground practice after the provincial government declared it illegal through Section 149 of the Indian Act passed in 1884. The village of Mamalilacula (also known as Meem

Quam Leese) was the site of a large, gift-giving ceremonial Kwakwaka'wakw potlatch in December of 1921.

It has been deserted since the 1960s, when the provincial government closed the school and moved all the people to Alert Bay. During the summers, Tom and his family care for the old site. Tom is a compelling storyteller, bringing to life the story of his people and the village named for the last potlatch. He claims that there were government spies present at that final potlatch celebration. Forty-five participants and tribal nobles were charged with offences such as making speeches, dancing, arranging to give articles away, and carrying gifts to recipients. Twenty-two people were sentenced to 2 - 6 month terms in Oakalla Prison in Burnaby. Tom's anguish over the shame and painful experiences of his people incarcerated in that frightening, confusing place was evident. Following the raid, ceremonial artefacts such as valuable coppers, sacred masks, rattles, and whistles were seized by the Alert Bay Indian Agent, William Halliday. Since then, many have been found in museums and private collections in Canada and the United States.

In 1980, the U'mista Cultural Centre at Alert Bay was completed to house the Potlatch Collection. Some of the once-lost items have been returned and are proudly displayed along with photographs of the original village, and works by Native artists, and films recounting the story of the potlatch.

As we sat among the totems carved with eagles, bears, whales, and other creatures who shared the land and sea, Tom's intoxicating monologue evoked the sound of drums, the stamping of dancing feet on dusty floors, and the scent of woodsmoke curling up through the longhouse roof during potlatch and other ceremonies. Tom's grandfather, author James Aul Sewid (Guests Never

Leave Hungry) was involved in negotiations to set the 200-mile international fishing limits for Canada. He travelled to Ottawa in 1964 while Vice President of the Native Brotherhood, a union representing Native fishermen and cannery workers. His former house still stands in the village, complete with its weathered grey cedar, tilting porch, and the sad eyes of broken windows looking out across the bay.

Bumblebees droned in the warm summer sun as we followed the little trails across the overgrown soccer pitch between the banks of blackberry blossoms. Seldom can I hurry past a bee. I love to follow them from bloom to bloom, noting their purposeful harvesting of pollen or nectar. But my lazy pursuit gets cut short by the decision to move along.

We chat with Tom's wife Kathleen, admire their baby and their yellow Lab named Land Claim. Kathleen recommends a camp on Turnour Island another mile or two away. She describes the area as a traditional one where Native women of the past harvested cedar bark for baskets, clothing and other objects.

We slid into our boats, gazing into the forest, imagining the People at work. We searched for signs of that ancient way of life. At dusk, an eagle silently drifted past us just over the water in evening mist – the sight reminded us of a Bateman painting.

The morning calm of July 29th was combined with radiation fog that burned off by nine o'clock, revealing a beautiful summer day. We launched into quiet water on an easterly course along Beware Channel, exploring the rocky nooks and taking photos of the numerous pictographs that can be seen when one looks carefully.

Because Beware Channel runs with a strong current, we worked eddies at every opportunity to make our distance down to Karlukwees, the deserted village site at the confluence of Beware and Clio Channels. Once round the point, the east wind picked up, and at lunchtime we rafted together to eat in a small bay halfway through Clio Channel. Five hours after we'd left camp, we pulled into Lagoon Cove on East Cracroft Island. Only a twelve-mile day, but one that was much more relaxed than the day before.

The people at Lagoon Cove Marina welcomed us warmly, inviting us to stay and camp on their lawn overlooking the cove. We eagerly accepted the camping offer, and paddled around to a beach with a safe spot for our kayaks and a gentle slope up to the lawn. We chose a spot with a shade tree, pitching our tents prior to exploring.

Several folks wanted to chat about the kayaks and our travels. We learned that our hosts have developed a loyal and annual pilgrim band of summer holidayers. We were just in time for 'Happy Hour' hosted by the marina. Participants are generally overnight moorage guests, but we were kindly included. Our hosts provided a big pot of cooked prawns with cocktail sauce, and the guests provided the balance of the food and liquid libations for the festive potluck event. We were determined to do our share, so Jaquie baked a pan of cornbread in double-quick time. Fresh, hot cornbread was a great hit and disappeared as quickly as the prawns and wine.

The evening turned out to be quite a party, with a combination of sailors, power boaters, marina staff, and kayakers gathered around a campfire singing along with the tunes strummed by the resident guitarist. We were very tempted to stay a second night, as this was one of the friendliest places we had encountered on our trip, but decided instead to move on.

We hadn't contacted home since leaving Waglisla nineteen days ago, and were looking for a telephone. We were due to check in with our families from Port Hardy or Telegraph Cove, but had by-passed both in favour of exploring the Broughton Archipelago, and our calls were overdue. One tends to wonder about the welfare of one's family while away on a long trip, and the urge for contact sometimes grows strong.

My mind went back to my Navy years in the sixties when I left my little family in New Zealand while I sailed for eight months at a time on Far East Station. The voyage took us to Fiji, Pearl Harbour, west across the Pacific to Hong Kong, Japan, Singapore, and Malaysia before returning through Indonesia, Australia, and home. Our only communication then was regular mail. How different things are now with the variety of media available for keeping in touch.

Although we didn't have a satellite phone for this journey, there are a few arguments for having such an option. It makes good sense from the risk management point of view, and safety margins can be widened considerably with such a device, no bigger than one of the original cellular phones.

In the morning we strolled along the dock, saying goodbye to all our new-found friends, and pausing to chat with a couple travelling in a fair-sized powerboat. They were quite apprehensive about Cape Caution, asking us how difficult it was to navigate. I was surprised when they have hundreds of horsepower at their disposal that they would ask kayakers. It seemed to me that they could just ease the throttle forward another notch and muscle through anything, but I admired them for erring on the side of caution. We gave them our observations, discussed wind/wave effects on the cape and they seemed readier to move on up the coast. Waving goodbye to the little group of observers, we dropped into our cockpits and headed for the 'Blow Hole'. This narrow channel threads its way from Lagoon Cove to Minstrel Cove Marina on Chatham Island and has a reputation for being a difficult passage.

We passed through with no trouble at all. Just around the corner we pulled into Minstrel Cove, where we took the opportunity to stock up with a few staples such as oatmeal and olive oil. The owner had no regular telephone service, but offered a cell phone so we could call home. An eagle sat watching from a tall tree. We were told that he lands there each day at this time, and that he's accustomed to scraps of meat and fish that get tossed to him from the restaurant kitchen. But we felt that the show was put on especially for us, and we marvelled again at the regal and powerful sight of this bird.

Satisfied that all was well in Vancouver, we ran down Chatham Channel at a fast clip. The five-knot current quickly popped us out into Hadley Bay then round to the south past Soderman Cove, a popular yachting destination, it seemed. The bay accommodated several boats at anchor. Jaquie paddled up to the *White Spruce*, a powerboat out of Seattle. The friendly crew of loungers informed her there were no services there, but offered us four cans of beer! *Thank you, White Spruce!*

We set out again, heading west down a winding route through Havannah Channel through sparkling, choppy water out to the confluence with Johnstone Strait. Now we were really in familiar territory. Johnstone Strait is the commuting route of the northern resident Orcas, and is populated by whale watching tours, cruise ships and tugs towing huge freight barges to Alaska and back. It's quite a highway, presenting a new and different challenge – traffic.

After an exhaustive search we found a beautiful beach camp at Domville Point just off the Broken Islands and decided the moment had come to try out the miniature crab trap again. After setting up camp, I paddled out to a likely looking spot, baited the cage with rockfish entrails, and dropped the trap in forty feet of water, anticipating an array of dangling crabs by morning. I tied the line to a yellow dry-bag to use as a buoy, then added a large rock for weight to keep the lot from drifting. Returning to camp, my mouth watered with visions of a crab feast.

Pasta carbonara with zucchini, red peppers and fried whole rockfish went down well as we contentedly watched the beautiful sunset in familiar country. We hadn't learned the names of the friendly crew who provided us the beer earlier, but while we savoured this libation, we were warmed again by the generosity of people we met.

We had chosen a typical beach camp, and once again carefully calculated the limit of the tide. At ten forty-five we peered out of our sleeping bags, and the water was within three feet of our tent as we'd calculated. Then the sea quietly receded, leaving our small part of the beach dry. We nodded off to sleep with the full moon shining on the nighttime calm of Johnstone Strait.

For breakfast I made coffee and oatmeal with apples. Then we packed and put in at nine o'clock in bright sunshine on a calm sea. Eager to retrieve our crabs, Mike was first out to the trap. When he came in sight of the line he yelled back, "You've caught a shark – I can see it on the bottom!"

I couldn't figure out how we could have caught a shark in such a tiny trap. We all converged on Mike, who handed me the buoy line. I hauled in the trap and sure enough, we could see a frightened little six-gill shark caught in one of the nooses surrounding the trap. Although it was barely two feet long, I was careful while pulling it up, grasping it behind the head, and gently releasing the noose that gripped it around the middle of its rough, sandpapery body. Placing the shark carefully back in the water, I held it a moment before I let it go. It seemed to fix me with a disgusted look as it rolled to look at me before heading to safety. I could almost hear it say, "You invited me for supper, but then made me stay all night in your stupid trap. What a dirty trick." The little fellow seemed to recover, and swam away with no visible damage. We still haven't had our crab feast.

Not to be defeated, Jaquie took over the trap and dropped it some distance away on a reef, while Mike jigged for rockfish close by. A few moments later, she pulled up the trap, ready to empty crabs into the cockpit of her boat. A large orange sunstar had emerged from the depths, hungrily wrapping itself around the tiny trap. It had completely enveloped the whole mechanism, its dozen or so tentacles trying unsuccessfully to get at the fish heads in the box. After carefully extricating our disappointing device from the predatory sunstar, we packed it up and moved on. We never did catch any crabs in the trap, but given the right territory it might perform in future.

Travelling east in Johnstone Strait along the main shipping lanes between the Strait of Georgia and the North Coast, our route was fairly straight. We cruised steadily along with the flood. But on reaching Stimpson Point, the easterly wind started to get up putting us in another 'wind against tide' situation where the waves shortened and steepened, making travel hard work. Lunch and a sprawl in the sun on the beach opposite Stimpson Reef felt welcome to our tired bodies.

We then slogged against the easterly for another two hours before pulling into Port Neville for a rest. The pleasant aspect of forest, the ancient greying timbers of the old buildings, and the homey sound of clucking hens greeted us. The homestead didn't appear to be a campsite, but we wanted to stay, so asked the woman in the store who graciously gave us permission. The grassy site was sheer luxury. We rigged the tarp to ward off the rain and dined on chili, cabbage and carrot salad with home made bread, followed by Jaquie's orange upside-down cake.

Jaquie:

We found the post office and old store – home now to the Beehive Mountain Gallery, a name that delighted me because I'm a beekeeper. Hans Hansen, a settler who arrived here from Norway in 1991 developed the homestead. He built his home and huts for visitors while clearing the land and fencing a garden with fruit trees. In November of 1895, he was sworn in as postmaster at Port Neville with a postal district stretching from Knight Inlet south to Loughborough Inlet. Prior to the building of a government dock in 1928, Union steam-

ships anchored in the bay while small boats pulled up to the cargo door to pick up mail and supplies. Two years later, Hansen married a widow with a young son, but he lost his wife barely a year later. He raised Willy during the next few years, but left him with a close friend when he returned to Norway where he met and married his second wife, Katrinka, who accompanied him to his West Coast home.

In 1920, Hansen began a two-storey log home, and was assisted by his friends and neighbours, using a hand-winch or block and tackle. This building became the post office, and their eldest daughter Karen was sworn in as postmistress. She later opened a large store, after the government built the large dock allowing steamships to unload freight. The store closed in 1960, but the post office has remained in service since 1895. This homestead has been in the Hansen family since 1891, and is still home to Laura, a granddaughter and her daughter.

The artist featured in the gallery, Peggy Sowden, lives across the bay, and is a keen kayaker. She was away from home, so we didn't get to meet her. I would have loved one of her paintings, but where to put it in a kayak? We set up the tents on the lawn behind the house and watched for the tame doe named Melody who apparently has just lost her fawn and has been huddled under a tree mourning for several days.

In the morning Jaquie purchased six fresh brown eggs laid by Lorna's hens, we filled up with our twenty-six litres of fresh water, and we were on the ocean by nine o'clock.

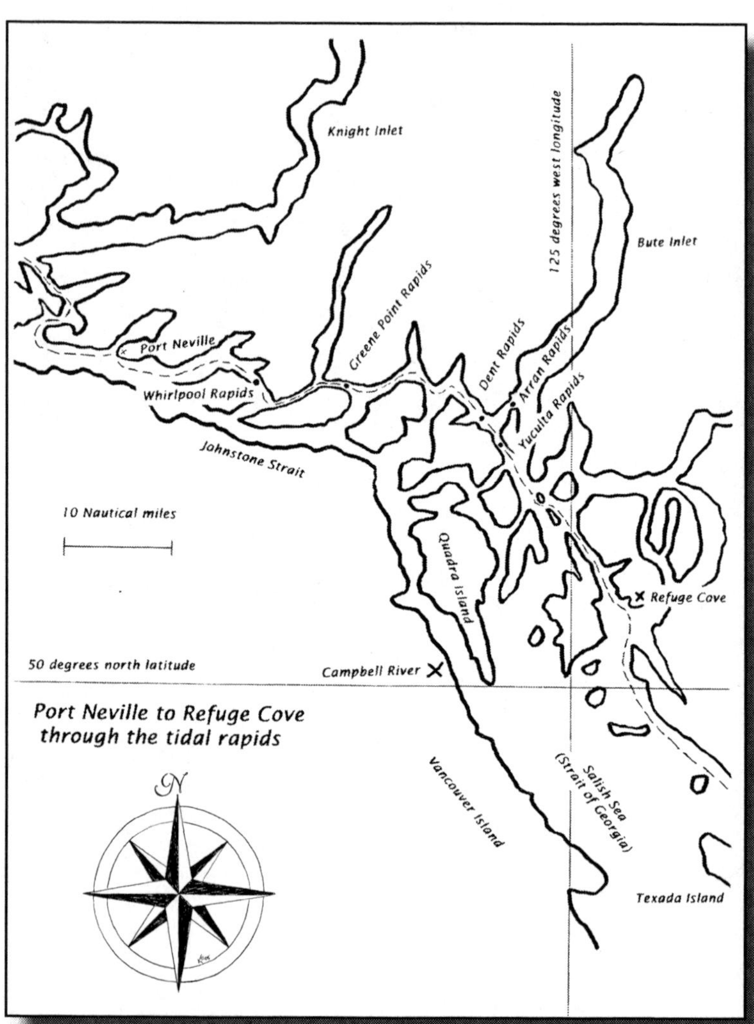
Knight Inlet
125 degrees west longitude
Bute Inlet
Greene Point Rapids
Port Neville
Dent Rapids
Arran Rapids
Yuculta Rapids
Whirlpool Rapids
Johnstone Strait
10 Nautical miles
Quadra Island
Refuge Cove
50 degrees north latitude
Campbell River
Port Neville to Refuge Cove
through the tidal rapids
N
Vancouver Island
Salish Sea
(Strait of Georgia)
Texada Island

CARE AND TIMING:

Canyons And Rapids

Every day since time began the sun, the moon, and the planets have been trying to pull the Pacific Ocean across the North American continent, then push it all back again. These massive forces of nature pit the sea against the land. In the short term, the land wins. The landforms compel the ocean to rush through the nip between Vancouver Island and the West Coast of Canada. Four times a day the huge tidal rapids change direction in a never-ending struggle to wear away the land and grind it into sediment. Ultimately, the ocean wins.

My lesson from all this is that we must temper the 'quick fix' mentality in our contemporary world and realize that we can only achieve big, meaningful things in life by persistence over time.

Often we set goals for ourselves and precisely nothing results. New Year's resolutions last a few short weeks. We attend seminars, retreats, read self-help books to learn how to set life goals. Then we have trouble remembering what the goals were, let alone how we're going to achieve them.

At other times we are unstoppable. Things happen effortlessly and success seems to fall into our hands. Calling it persistence and self-discipline is not enough. Something far deeper must determine our will to succeed. Perhaps it's related to our belief systems, our images of who and what we are, a feeling that this is our major purpose. Identify that major purpose and you have the Midas touch. With the vision set firmly in mind, the 'go' feeling in our hearts, the process will automatically produce the results we visualized.

Six miles later we entered Sunderland Channel and a world of wind and pouring rain. We were still moving east towards the series of four tidal rapids we would traverse before entering Desolation Sound. Although it was summer time we were wearing our wetsuits, polypropylene tops, fleece jackets, paddling jackets, and wool hats as we plugged our way across the water. Hot soup helped ward off the cold and wet as we made a lunch stop opposite Seymour Island on the south side of the channel.

Another five miles and nearly three hours saw us at a camp in the dark forest on Wellbore Channel, right at the entrance to Whirlpool Rapids. We were now well positioned for the morning slack the next day. During the evening we painstakingly calculated our launch time for our passage through Whirlpool.

The standard approach for most of these rapids is to be positioned in an eddy thirty minutes before the turn. As you push into the narrows against the last of the current you feel it diminish down to three knots… two knots… one knot as it prepares to turn and then it will take you through. The window of opportunity for most sea kayakers is very narrow, six minutes or less is typical. Variables include the length of the passage, the ability and fitness of the group, the maximum speed of the flood or ebb, the time of year, whether it is the big tide change or the small change of the day, and the barometric pressure. We scout out the rapids from land if there is a safe little nook close by. If we are able to scramble up a hill above the rapid, we can better judge the distance to the crux of the channel before we set out. While adrenaline-seeking whitewater kayakers will look for the fastest currents and the biggest overfalls, most long distance travellers with their heavily-laden boats will go to great pains to take advantage of the slack water.

As we prepared to depart at 5:45 the next morning, the dark of the forest and the rain made it look like night. Speech came in monosyllables and grunts as we rubbed sleep out of our eyes in the gloomy grey dawn. Knowing we had eaten all of our quick lunch food, I baked some bannock while we ate a little breakfast. The carry was a difficult one. We had a low tide, and the downpour on the kelp made the boulders extremely slippery. But we were committed to being in the water and away as fast as possible.

Soon the four of us were poised in the eddy to the north of Carterer Point, 15 minutes before the turn. We watched the last of the ebb run to the north past us. Then as it slowed, stopped, and turned, we pushed out into the flood and gently picked up speed as we cruised through Whirlpool Rapids on the building tide.

The three-mile run down to D'Arcy Point was pure bliss, riding on a calm with lazy strokes and – the biggest treat of all – seeing our first arbutus tree while rounding D'Arcy Point. While this may not sound remarkable to everyone, the arbutus is the signature tree of the Strait of Georgia and the Gulf Islands. How many hundreds of nights have we slept under the familiar arbutus on a warm summer night while cruising the Gulf Islands and the San Juan Islands! This was a benchmark on our trip, signalling our passage into southern waters.

Accompanied by a small school of porpoises we crossed the one-mile wide Chancellor Channel and pulled into camp just before the rain began. Our aim was to set up for the next day's run through Greene Point Rapids. Unfortunately, when approaching from the west, Greene Point has a three-mile long run against the ebb. This meant that for three miles before reaching the narrows we would be in a tide race, either with or against, depending on how we timed it. We knew there would be a few eddies to take advantage of, but no significant refuge. We chose the confluence of Loughborough Inlet and Chancellor Channel as our home for the night, and we would do some meticulous planning to determine how best to cover our three miles to Greene Point the next morning. The day's run was only eight miles, but progress here is determined by nature, not by human-powered boats.

Five-thirty came and we were out of our sleeping bags having a quick breakfast, and then we were into the water. Progress to the east towards Greene Point was a combination of quick bursts around the points and slow drifts close in towards the wall in back eddies. Often in these waterways you can't get close enough to the wall to take maximum advantage of eddies, due to the thick kelp that tangles up paddles and boats in its heavy fronds and stems. Sometimes we found a thin line of open water right under the wall where the tides and surf keep the kelp off the rocks, but these thin leads often come up to a dead end, leaving a kayaker forced to push, thrash, and slide the hull over a dense bed of kelp.

Our party actually reached Greene Point early, and spent the extra time exploring the rock walls along the south side of the channel. The sea life here, as in any channel that is constantly flushed by strong currents, was prolific. There were many "oohs" and "aahs" as we watched the feeding efforts of hundreds of small creatures.

As the ebb died down to three knots, we started our push through the rapids proper. Once again we timed it to cruise through on the turn, hugging the south side of the channel to the corner of Mayne Passage. We then took a fast two-mile mid-channel run straight down to Lorte Island and pulled up at the German restaurant at Cordero Lodge. My friend and fellow kayaker, Matthew Smith, had raved about the bratwurst he'd enjoyed there when soloing this route two years previously.

The restaurant opened at 11:30 precisely. We tied up at the float, stripped off our wetsuits, and made ourselves as presentable as possible while anticipation made us all a little crazy, and induced some delicious delusions. As soon as the doors were unlocked, four smelly kayakers rushed to a table and attempted to eat the place out of food. Of course we didn't succeed, but the attempt was impressive, and included lots of coffee in real ceramic cups instead of our ususal plastic mugs with a history of the world's coffee occupying the bottom. If you can tell the age of a tree by the rings in the wood, I swear you can tell the years of wilderness travellers' experience by the stains in their coffee mugs.

Our feast included meaty European sausage, German potato salad and red cabbage, thick slices of bread smeared with real butter. When our appetites and enthusiasm were satisfied we ordered strudel and more coffee. We groaned with pleasure, then reluctantly pushed ourselves up from the table and waddled out onto the float.

We put in and rode the remainder of the flood east for three and a half miles in the bright sunshine to Thurlow Bay. This old settlement is beautifully preserved. It has a government dock, but no facilities for boaters. A stroll along the boardwalk was a pleasant contrast to the hours of paddling. Even in camp, unless there happens to be a surf beach, walking is often restricted to a few yards of stumbling over rocks.

The afternoon wind was getting up, so we untied from the dock and struggled into the funnelling southeaster. Anxious to position ourselves for Dent and Yaculta, the rapids we intended to traverse the next day, we aimed for the easterly tip of East Thurlow Island. It took all our strength to paddle against the gap wind between Channel Island and East Thurlow. Mike landed to check out a likely camp on the north side of the tiny peninsula at Johns Point while Sara, Jaquie, and I circled round to the small beach on the east side.

Luckily, the three of us found an ideal camp high above the beach. Mike joined us as we explored the tenting possibilities. We built a kitchen on a terraced flat spot that had a view of the sheltered bay below us. By the time we had unpacked the boats, the shoreline was strewn with wet gear tied to branches and logs. The easterly was still blowing hard and the wind dried our all our gear in no time. Leftover stew, bannock, and cornbread made a great supper, and we spent the evening rechecking the calculations for navigating through Dent and Yaculta the next day.

Jaquie:

All along the trip I'd been supplementing our diet with whatever edible plants we encountered. I'd seen salal just beginning to bloom as we passed south of Prince Rupert, and I'd looked forward to browsing on the berries later in the summer. We haven't yet found Labrador tea, although I have no doubt that it has been all around us. No doubt if I had looked more carefully, I'd have found it. Wild onion has been a welcome addition to our pasta sauce, and fresh mint from the rocky bank behind the Big House in Kitkatla made a tasty hot tea with honey.

Here on the windy point just before the entrance to Dent, Rick has built me a great kitchen with a lovely view over the water. I've found a few ripe salal berries and we picked a few to pop into our mouths. I long for fresh strawberries warm from the sun, and raspberries over ice cream. At home the Okanagan cherries would now be appearing in all the fruit stands. The dried apricots, plums, pears, apples and raisins that I occasionally stew for breakfast or dessert help to fill my love of fruit, but this summer I am missing the glorious bounty of the south. My eye is on sunny, south-facing banks where wild strawberries might grow. No salmon berries or blackberries grow this far north, but we are steadily working our way south.

We had considerable doubts about launching the next morning, as the wind was still strong. We decided to alter our route slightly, minimizing the effects of windage on the boats and put in at eight o'clock. Our timing had to be exact for Dent and Yaculta, and any delay would mean no attempt for maybe three days. We'd calculated the turn at Dent for eleven in the morning. This would be perfect for our passage today because we were setting out early enough to miss the worst of the easterly wind that blew up around noon. It's highly inadvisable to try traversing to the east through Dent into the wind. The times of the high and low slacks step forward by about fifty minutes each day, which would put the next day's turn at noon, just in time for the easterly. In addition to this, a storm had been predicted to come through any time in the next twenty-four hours. So we were highly motivated to get through that day, spurred on by the thought of sleeping between clean sheets if we could make the fishing resort at Big Bay.

Rushing nature is usually a recipe for danger. In New Zealand many years ago I clearly remember watching the television news, seeing a news clip of two shrouded bodies being carried out of the mountains on stretchers. It was only the next day that their names were announced. I remember the hammer-blow I felt in my stomach when I learned they were two of my closest mountaineering friends. Bruce and Irene were found roped together, drowned after an unsuccessful river crossing in the Southern Alps, probably hurrying to warmth and comfort after a hard climb. Such lessons during my years in mountain search and rescue have taught me the mark of a wilderness traveller is not so much being able to move fast through difficult terrain as having the ability to stay put, patiently waiting out a storm, and making yourself comfortable – physically, mentally, and spiritually.

The ability to sit down and wait for a week has saved my skin on a few occasions – both in mountains and on the water in many parts of the world. All these things went through my mind as we battled in a big arc, fighting both the wind and the powerful ebb from Dent. I would rather call it off and camp in safety rather than be seduced by that hot shower, those clean sheets or that beer and burger.

We reached Gomer Island at nine o'clock after a particularly circuitous route, partly veering into Frederick Arm to avoid the worst of the ebb. The rock wall on the east side of Gomer was taking the brunt of the current from Dent, and the reflected waves gave us a rough ride until we slipped into the calm of the three-mile bay leading up to Horn Point. I had almost resigned myself to the fact that we would miss today's turn, because we had lost a lot of time in our initial approach to Dent. Horn Point is difficult to round against the ebb if you arrive more than an hour before the turn. Due mainly to Mike's drive and determination, when we reached Horn Point we weren't too far behind schedule. We rounded it at ten o'clock and, paddling as hard as we could, just managed to creep around into the eddy beyond.

Jaquie: (mid-day)

What a day. The hearty oatmeal breakfast served us well. The tension surrounding the timing and technique involved in these rapids has built up to an almost visible level. Conversation is terse, short, and mostly involves charts, currents and the weather. My enjoyment of the journey has reached a low point, and I recognize my weak navigation skills are the cause. My heart is in the life and beauty around me, not in the details derived by man.

We paddle single file around the points and through the eddies along the rock walls. Mike leads around Horn Point. I follow, paddling at maximum strength in order to just make way. Sara is too close behind me and hits my rudder; my kayak loses ground and momentum. I'm panicked thinking I'll go over while I struggle to regain balance and keep my bow into the current. We need to give each other more wiggle room to correct for error without dangerous collisions.

Our track took us onto the large-scale hydrographic charts of Dent and Yaculta. These charts show the behaviour of the currents hour by hour in the Dent-Arran-Yaculta Basin – extremely valuable information. What had seemed unattainable became a simple matter of navigating the predicted current directions through to Gillard Passage and Big Bay. We paddled between Dent and Little Dent Islands, and across the basin to Gillard Passage as the wind picked up, slowing us down noticeably. The flood took us round the north side of Jimmy Judd Island and we headed across the current in Gillard Passage to Big Bay.

Mike and Sara were a few minutes ahead of us, already drifting in the eddy off Hessler Point. The current rapidly built up speed in the few minutes between the pairs of boats, and meant that Jaquie and I had to ferry hard left to make it across the hundred-foot wide tide race and into the same eddy. I screamed, "Paddle! Paddle hard!" as she seemed to be slipping back. I couldn't watch both her and my line in the current at the same time, but I was afraid she wouldn't make it, and be gone out through the next rapid.

We were swept two hundred yards downstream, crossing one hundred yards of fast moving water, straining at our paddles. Gradually we each pulled out of the fierce current into the outside edge of the back eddy and rested, eyes wide with the knowledge of our near miss. We floated a few minutes to catch our breath, then drifted up to the resort in flat calm.

There was space to tie up and unload our gear right on the dock. Big Bay Marina Lodge had a two-bedroom suite miraculously vacant for us so we booked for two nights of well-deserved R & R.

Laundry, clean clothes, hot showers, restaurant meals, chairs to sit in, beds to climb into, and phone calls home all contributed to a completely different world. Ironically, the hotel room at the resort was the only place where a wild animal got into our food cache. We had been fanatically disciplined about protecting our food all the way from Alaska, but short of hanging it from the chandelier, I'd decided to leave the food in our big carry bag on the floor at the foot of the bed. In the early hours of the morning I was awakened by scrabbling noises in our food. I jumped out of bed, opened the bag, and started to toss out the food, determined to find the culprit. Sure enough, a little grey mouse popped out and dashed under the bed. Jaquie joined the pursuit and after a few circuits of the room, the little guy disappeared down a hole next to the bathtub.

Jaquie: (evening)

Civilization has hit us with a palpable force. We shower in hot water with soap that produces suds. What effect will this have as it drains into the bay? We eat snack foods wrapped in plastic and toss the wrapper away into a trash bin. Where will it go? How long will it exist in some landfill? How much fossil fuel is burned to heat our spacious room, the restaurant, and the retail shop? In Rick's courses, he sometimes does an exercise which measures, in square miles, the ecological footprint of individuals in different cultures. How much has our footprint increased while staying in this lap of luxury?

During the evening, the yacht Nova Spirit *cruises in,*

docking for the night. We admire its beauty and lavishness, giggling as we compare our lifestyle to that of the passengers who have been traveling aboard this floating luxury hotel. As they disembark onto the float and drift towards us in their fancy evening attire, we're sharply reminded of the salty rime on our faces, and the 'Eau d'Ocean' hanging around us like fog. We meet and converse, suggesting to the curious guests that a kayak is a 'real' boat!

My longing for family is assuaged. A call to my son fills in the gaps with bits of news of the grandbabies, jobs, and accomplishments. With slightly misty eyes I hang up the phone and look out over the tops of the fibreglass monsters in the bay to the tall dark trees beckoning me across the channel. Tomorrow will be another adventure.

Our rest period over, we were eager to make passage into Desolation Sound via Calm Channel. The turn to flood at Yuculta (pronounced Yukkatah) wouldn't occur until noon and so packing was a leisurely affair. The resort staff transported our gear down to our kayaks in a trailer pulled by a small quad ATV. I might have been overheard muttering that all beaches should be equipped with one.

The exit from Big Bay was so easy. As we pulled out into the current 'train' in Gillard Passage, it picked up speed and we picked up an entourage of about fifty curious seals. They looked like a huge field of footballs scattered across the Channel, with more and more gathering behind us as we scooted along with the speeding current. Where there are seals there are fish, so Jaquie trolled a buzz bomb and it wasn't long before she had a salmon on board. Sadly, it was undersized and covered with sea lice. After picking off several of the lice, she put it back into the water. We watched Whirlpool Point, Kellsey Point, and

Harbott Point slip silently by in sequence on our left. In no time at all, the 'train' in Calm Channel slowed. We paddled down to Bassett Point, which marks the east exit to Hole-in-the-Wall. It was now full flood out of Hole-in-the-Wall, and we were expecting to be punched to the east, but were surprised to feel absolutely no current at all as we passed close in.

The Rendezvous Islands were in view, and we made good time crossing to the northern tip of the group. Sara and I had camped there about ten years earlier, and we headed directly to the spot we remembered. This would be the last the four of us would travel together, as Sara and Mike had decided to push on ahead of us down the coast to Vancouver.

Having cleared the last of the big rapids, our mood was relaxed. For the first time since leaving the Alaska border we were south of all significant obstacles. I reminded myself of the seductive *laissez-faire* attitude that can lead to danger if you think all the hazards are behind you. I have accidentally dropped my ice axe while walking down the trail through the bush after a climb. Since I have never dropped my ice axe during a climb, I've come to the conclusion that an alert, competent person is safer in a dangerous situation than a person with a carefree attitude in a relatively safe situation. That night we celebrated our journey in good company, celebrating with a happy hour of fried oysters, seafood sauce, and red wine.

In the morning we bade farewell to Mike and Sara. They headed off down through Lewis Channel towards Desolation Sound and home, and would arrive five days before us. Jaquie and I packed slowly and launched later that morning in beautiful summer sunshine, heading toward Teakerne Arm and Desolation Sound.

In the early afternoon a massive school of porpoises passed us from left to right, coming out of Teakerne Arm and heading towards Cortez Island. The school was so big we could still see them moving out of sight to the west as more continued to appear from the east. We watched them cutting through the water as far south as we could see, some of them spy-hopping like Orcas, something we hadn't seen porpoises do before. The whole channel was alive with these amazing animals, and we snapped shot after shot as they passed.

Looking south we saw the Comox Glacier on Vancouver Island, glistening in the sun. A compass bearing helped to locate a small, secluded beach camp we'd used with friends on a past trip. We closed around the headland and found the beach, but it was crowded with kayaks so we moved south another mile or so to a tiny surge channel. We ran in, pulled our boats onto a rock shelf, and discovered the most amazingly perfect camp. A small time spent gardening made our home fit to move right into, and there was even time to enjoy a spectacular sunset while our supper was cooking. Now utterly relaxed and content, we felt the warmth of home territory, familiar country stretching ahead right down the Strait of Georgia.

Jaquie:

In many camps we intruded into the fishing territory of the belted Kingfishers. Looking as though they're dressed up in white collars and black ties with formal dinner jackets, they perch on tree limbs several feet above the water, watching for the movement of small fish. Dropping straight down into the water, they emerge with a little silvery flopping prize, then take up their perch again, working to align the fish for easy swallowing. Their distinctive scolding call is instantly recognizable. But we never noticed the pellets they cough up like owls – the indigestible parts of the fish, crab, clams, or insects they eat. I resolve to spend more time investigating under their favourite perches.

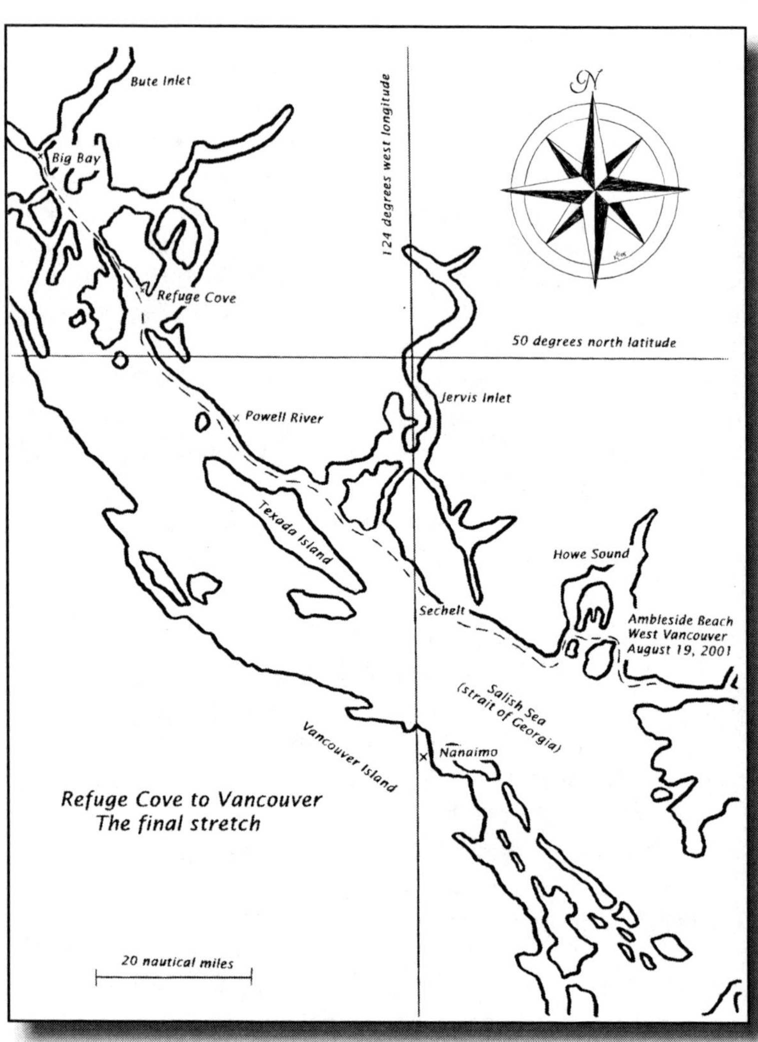
Bute Inlet
Big Bay
Refuge Cove
124 degrees west longitude
N
50 degrees north latitude
Powell River
Jervis Inlet
Texada Island
Howe Sound
Sechelt
Ambleside Beach
West Vancouver
August 19, 2001
Salish Sea
(strait of Georgia)
Vancouver Island
Nanaimo
Refuge Cove to Vancouver
The final stretch
20 nautical miles

ISLANDS

...deepest depths of heart and soul
feelings yearning to be consoled
shrouded in the drifting mists
as gentle as a touch of lips...
a kiss as soft as a whisper
of secrets told...
...then the mists begin to lift
and we behold
our islands aren't so desolate as before
I guess that's what friends are really for.

Sunshine and the Smell of Home:

The Strait of Georgia

Fifty-three days out and we're still thoroughly enjoying every single day. This has been one of the most consistently pleasant journeys I have ever done. Every day is unique – from the scenery to the wildlife to the people we have met. But then it has been a 'designer trip' from the outset. Low daily mileage, coupled with the ten spare days, has ensured the success of our basic goal – to live on the coast.

What are the basic ingredients for enjoyment? Is it derived from our own outlook, from our own philosophy? Does it depend on outside influences like weather, the people we are with, the variety and pleasure of outside experiences? If we had allowed the weather to dominate our spirits we would have been miserable for over a third of the journey. No matter what the situation, we possess the power to choose our attitude.

The high-pressure ridge continued to smile on us as we launched from Surge Channel Camp in bright sunshine again on August 8th, Day Fifty-three. We'd savoured our journey as the days had progressed. With all the major challenges behind us, our relaxed mood continued. Another hour took us into Refuge Cove for the culture shock of an all-too-real contact with summer tourism. Everywhere we looked, plastic boats criss-crossed our path. No one waved a neighbourly greeting as they had along the North Coast. Desolation Sound in summer is noisy and redolent with diesel fumes. I don't know who named it, but whoever it was couldn't have conceived what it would look like in the twenty-first century, as 'desolate' it's not!

We landed at Refuge Cove to pick up supplies, and while I wandered about the store I spied a box of granola bars. The shop was quite crowded with holiday-makers. As I squeezed through the lineup, excusing myself, I reached up to the granola bars. Jaquie, who had been watching, suggested, "Not those, they're low fat. We need the fats!" A couple looked at us in utter horror as if to say, "Are you crazy?" We did indeed need as many calories as possible, but this was a surprisingly difficult task in a shop full of processed snacks filled with preservatives and artificial sweeteners. Jaquie was conscious of preparing meals with the caloric energy we needed without sacrificing other beneficial nutrients that would keep our immune systems healthy and strong.

Since the beginning of the trip it seemed that I had been eating anything I could lay my hands on. Still, I had lost fifteen pounds and was getting used to feeling hungry much of the time. Oh, that I could eat and exercise like this while I work in Vancouver! This fit, lean, healthy feeling is something to be treasured. We never did buy those granola bars, but hit the pastry shop for fresh scones with apricots and walnuts instead.

Jaquie:

We posed on beaches that came to resemble multi-coloured flower beds – littered as they were with red, yellow, blue and green dry bags clustered around our sleeping and working areas. Many times teeny, zippy hummingbirds and big fat, lazy bumblebees would fly about from one bag to another, as if unable to believe something so colourful could be anything but a blossom – a source of nectar and pollen – in an environment mostly bichromatic green and brown. Once as we sat in the shade under a leafy tree, we observed a family of Rufous hummingbirds feeding two fledglings that hopped up and down on little branches, hovering and begging for food. We welcomed the telltale zzzt-zzzt announcing their presence over our heads.

In Refuge Cove there was a beekeeper selling jars of his local honey. I simply had to purchase some, and was as always, drawn into conversation with a colleague. We chatted about the floral source of his golden wares and I discovered that his largest source is blackberry blossoms. Wild flowers produce a honey like none other, fragrant with suggestive notes of berries and maple. Tasting honeys from exotic places is similar to tasting fine wines. Experienced beekeepers can pick out various floral sources that tell a story of the summer travels of the busy bees.

The surface of the sea across the mouth of Desolation Sound was mirror-like and the weather continued sunny, so different from an average day on the North Coast. It felt like the tropics by comparison. This was the Strait of Georgia, and we jockeyed our way among the many boaters past Kinghorn Island and around Sara Point at the top of the Malaspina Peninsula. Rhythmically paddling down past Bliss Landing, we pulled into a favourite camp in the Copeland Islands Marine Park. Amazingly, there was no one else in residence.

We set up our tent fifty feet above a burnished bronze sea on a perfect summer afternoon. The feeling of being on home territory was strong within us. We swam in the balmy clear water before supper. The fried oysters in garlic, pasta, and a glass of red wine were rounded out by an apple upside-down cake. After nine lazy miles today, we wandered off to bed on the Sunshine Coast.

Pleased that the gentle nor'wester and the high-pressure ridge were still being kind to us, we launched in the morning and pushed on to Lund. After coffee and a cinnamon bun at the bakery, we moved south, and twelve miles later were in Powell River, passing the massive structure of the mill. We pulled into a marina near the Comox-Powell River ferry dock and called our friend, Caroline. She arrived with her truck and trailer to pick us up. Kayaks and contents were unloaded from the water and reloaded onto the trailer; soon we were installed at Caroline's home for supper and a good visit. While we feasted on carrots and tomatoes fresh from her garden we caught up on the news of the province, and Caroline asked for stories of our trek.

The three days at Powell River were the longest rest we'd had on the whole journey, and we thoroughly enjoyed the hospitality and change of environment. We carried out boat maintenance and equipment repairs, went for early morning walks, visited a farm to help feed the horses, swam and enjoyed doing things on land for a while.

On our second rest morning we explored the neighbourhood and visited in the kitchen while Caroline baked some fragrant applesauce cakes and cookies. In the afternoon we toured a freshwater salmon hatchery on a lake northeast of town. The one million fish raised there are started on January 1st each year, thriving at a temperature of 20 degrees Celsius. They begin their lives in large tanks, and at a certain point are transferred to pens in the lake. We learned that they are prone to fungal and bacterial diseases for which they are treated, but sea lice aren't a problem for them in the fresh water of the lake. Antibiotics are used to treat for bacterial diseases, and we tried to imagine the technicians injecting the individual fish with the medication. *A slippery business indeed.*

Three days were enough for us to get restless again for the ocean and the journey. Even as we thanked Caroline and her family for their hospitality we looked forward to the motion of the sea and to the discipline of the journey. Falling into the familiar rhythm of the water and the paddles, we journeyed through the Malaspina Strait with Texada Island on our right.

Our boats had been our home for fifty-eight days and this had become more of a lifestyle than a trip, just as we'd hoped for it to be from the outset. My kayak had taken on a character and a personality of its own. It was solid, accepting, stable – in no way skittish, just utterly reliable.

I have owned three kayaks in eighteen years and the Seafarer has taken me further and longer than any other. I feel the stress in the hull every time I'm forced to abuse it on rough landings, gouging pullouts and crashes on sharp rocks. My first boats were West Greenland designs: rudderless, with tiny cockpits and straight full-length keels to keep them running straight in heavy seas. The Nimbus Seafarer is a Pacific Northwest style of kayak with higher volume. It has a large cockpit and a hefty rudder, invaluable in a following sea. It is a great expedition and guide boat, and I took a long time to evaluate similar boats before choosing it. Aesthetically, it falls short of some of the beautiful craft I see on the water, but its characteristics make it ideal for my purposes. It carries heavy loads, is sturdy enough to haul people out of the water and up on deck, and always comes up smiling. During the search for 'my' boat I had been tempted by sleeker, beautifully arced boats with technical quick-turn capabilities. However, many of my long-distance wilderness friends in the sea kayak community preferred the Seafarer — a quiet, unobtrusive, unspectacular craft that always got them there and, more importantly, always got them home. It is true that a kayak is only as good as its paddler, but the team is enhanced with the right craft.

We were moving west past Albion Point, Brew Bay, Lang Bay, Frolander Bay, and finally pulling in at Scotch Fir Point on Jervis Inlet for the night. Jervis Inlet is the second ferry crossing on the highway up the Sunshine Coast, a route we often travel on our forays up to Desolation Sound, but how different everything looks from the sea. Holiday homes are interspersed with quiet bushy areas, but to our delight, there are still a few secluded beaches.

Scotch Fir Camp proved as pleasant as the 'best' one on the Copeland Islands. A crescent beach faced west, and there was a good landing and launch area for our kayaks. And there was all that sun-warmed water for lazy swims every few hours. Who could want anything more in this simple life we were leading? In the setting sun we ate our fajitas, and made a toast to Texada Island with a mug of red wine. As we sprawled out, basking in a balmy summer twilight, the stars appeared one by one above our drowsy heads.

The morning sun woke us up on August 13th, with only six days to go. Jaquie made a litre of clam chowder with the mahogany clams she'd dug fresh from the pebble beach.

As we waited for the high tide we ate our brunch of poached eggs on focaccia bread. After an eleven-thirty launch, we crossed Jervis Inlet to Alexander Point on Hardy Island, with no drift at high slack. Another three hours and the ebb would have forced us to ferry into Nelson Island to avoid being pushed out into Malaspina Strait.

Jaquie:

Shellfish were infrequent in our diet, as we weren't confident that we could accurately judge PSP or shellfish poisoning by the numbness test (rubbing a bit of the flesh over a lip, waiting for numbness or tingling to indicate 'red tide'). One camp on a thin spit was an exception. As the tide rolled back, revealing a vast field of oysters, I got out my fish knife and went to work on a few. No lip tingle, so they became a scrumptious appetizer before our dinner. Yum.

One evening we made camp in a small shallow bay. At low tide that evening I noticed it was a very promising clam beach. Early the next morning the sandy beach was alive with clam spouts, and I was off to dig! With a bowl of them harvested, the pot went onto the stove to brew our hearty chowder. The last of the onion, a carrot, a couple of chopped cabbage leaves, and a bit of salt and pepper combined with some sun-dried tomatoes went in with the fresh clams. We dined well, with enough left over for seconds.

Along the mainland shore we passed several quarries that had obviously been worked some years earlier. Texada Island has a huge limestone industry, and maybe these were satellite limestone quarries. We imagined that the grit in our toothpaste might have come from our very own coastal quarries. Feeling silly, the thought made us flash cheesy smiles at each other. The commercial traffic in the strait now includes barges of limestone heading to plants all over the west coast.

The number of pleasure boats was increasing. A smoky blue haze hung over the water, the smell of engine oil diminishing the pleasure of our travel. Slicing through the clear water, my mind wandered. I started thinking that there are too many of us concentrated in pleasure-pockets now. If, in the vastness of Nunavut you see a snowmobile crossing the vast winter landscape, you greet the traveller and stop – maybe for a night, or just for a chat and a cup of tea. But you always stop to visit. There may only be the two of you within a hundred miles. It's a great event to see another person and a pleasure to swap news or discuss the weather. If you are hurt, or out of food, it's literally a lifesaver. One snowmobile makes little impact on the land. A hundred years ago one person felling a tree would make little impact on the land. There weren't enough of us then to do significant damage to these wild places, nor did we have the technology to alter the face of the earth at our present breath-taking rate.

Nelson Island slid slowly by on our left side and we approached Agamemnon Channel. We knew we would be unlikely to find a wilderness camp along this shore, lined as it was with wall-to-wall with cottages, so we crossed to the throat of Agamemnon and made for Pender Harbour. This picturesque tangle of tiny waterways and islands allows glimpses of delightful retreats. Cottages surrounded by the toys and trivia of holidays provide bright splashes of colour in the afternoon sunlight. The freshening nor'wester pushed us into Irvine's Landing, where we enjoyed a meal at the pub before making inquiries about a place to stay for the night. Our server directed us along to Duncan Cove where we found a tent site in the campground. It seemed a travesty to pay sixteen dollars for such a little patch of dried up, dusty grass, but we put the shower and store to good use before we enjoyed a good night's sleep.

August 14th – We awakened to the now-familiar high-pressure ridge. It had accompanied us since Big Bay on Day Fifty-two, eight days earlier. The summer had been everything we could have hoped for during our transit down the Strait of Georgia. The forecast predicted twenty knots from the northwest by evening, so we anticipated a fast ride to Buccaneer Bay.

While we made breakfast, Jaquie baked a loaf of bread for lunch, and we left camp as soon as it had cooled sufficiently to pack. A quick burst took us round the corner to a store in Pender Harbour, where we bought a block of cheese. We then threaded our way through the narrow gap behind Francis Peninsula and headed out for the seven-mile stretch to North Thormanby

Island. The run down the coast was a rhythmic three hours of paddling along a straight coastline that presented no navigational problems.

It was a good time to think and I mentally drifted back. As the miles slipped easily past, I found memories of places in the mountains and on the seas re-running through my mind like old movies. I derive pleasure in revisiting the things that really matter to me. Survival, life, death, people, loved ones – not phones, email, a pile of papers crying, "Me! Do me! Me!" *Boy, I'm going to make some changes when I get home.* How could a pile of mere paper create stress? We humans must be crazy!

As the sandstone cliffs of North Thormanby gradually grew taller on the southern horizon, I began to drift back to reality. We bore to the west and took the direct line into the funnel of Buccaneer Bay. Our timing was perfect, landing at four o'clock right on the top of the highest tide of the day. We stepped out of our boats onto the sand at Grassy Point Camp. The carry was short and easy. We pitched the tent in that beautiful pastel of late afternoon, when everything appears softened by a northwest haze as though shot through a filtered lens. Grassy Point has a northerly aspect looking toward the Northern Sunshine Coast. It's a favourite venue for training courses in the Sea Kayak Association of B.C. Countless times I've sat late into the evening on this very point with close friends, recounting stories and dreaming of adventures to come. Jaquie and I spread out a little more than our habit, perhaps overdue for a break, and savoured the chowder from Scotch Fir Point with a loaf of freshly baked bread.

We were a day ahead of our scheduled arrival at Vancouver. The decision to spend two nights at Buccaneer Bay was reached with ease. Our rest day that followed was very entertaining, watching the antics of day-trippers in their watercraft, their ingenious ways of anchoring and getting the in-laws on and off the boat without wet feet. Our personal entertainment was reading, eating, studying the wildlife, taking beach walks, and doing all those 'nothing' things that a day at the beach is supposed to be. The sun on our skin induced a delicious laziness that slowed the passage of time and sank deep into our souls.

Jaquie:

The sun is brilliant yet again. We wandered among the multitude of watercourses to exit Pender Harbour, and after just over three easy hours of paddling, pulled out on Grassy Point. It looked busy at mid-afternoon, but by dusk there were only four camping parties in sight. Next to us is an encampment decked out with Coleman stove, gas lantern, and coolers packed with copious amounts of beer and wine. A young blonde woman accompanies three upwardly mobile male youths. Their fire grows larger as darkness falls, leading my cynical side to believe they are afraid of the dark. The glare of their lantern eliminates the gentle starlight, and we slide into our tent hoping they will revel quietly. For the next hour or more, wood smoke wafts unpleasantly into the tent and I resolve to turn it 90 degrees tomorrow to avoid some of the drifting smoke if they are indeed settled for the duration.

Some time in the early hours I woke up to delicious silence. I crawled out of the tent quietly and stood under a brilliant sky full of falling stars with a waning moon just over the eastern hill. The air is fresh again after the neighbours' bonfire has burned down, and the sunburnt grass is fragrant under my feet. I crawled back into my sleeping bag to return to dreams.

Rick has rigged the tarp for shade here on the open beach. We sit in our little 'chairs' reading, snacking, musing. A little bird spends the afternoon with us, often coming within just a few inches of us, prompting Rick to name him. 'Henry' is greyish, with speckles or bars, lighter tan on his throat and breast. He has a short, broad back with a streamlined small head and dark feet. We tempted him with crumbs, but he prefers the abundant grasshoppers and other insects he finds quite near our idyll. I think he may be a water pipit.

The next day we woke up to overcast and wind. Our high-pressure ridge had come abruptly to an end. We launched at ten o'clock, and as we turned to the south into the maw of the seemingly ironically-named Welcome Passage, we could feel eighteen knots from the south, combined with three knots of flood moving in the same direction. The passage can present a classic 'gap' wind where the wind is compressed through a narrow pass or between islands, increasing its speed. A tug towing a log boom was fighting its way south into the passage, travelling at less than half a knot. We waited in a nook for half an hour for it to pass, unwilling to cross in front of it.

Eventually we paddled half a mile north, crossed behind the tug, and tucked into Smuggler's Cove for lunch. The wind speed had increased, and the sea state had worsened by the time we came out again. We passed the tug on the east side, and started our transit of Welcome Passage. We paddled harder than we had on the whole trip, but barely made any headway. Unable to keep up the pace any longer, we finally took shelter halfway through the passage. We baked bannock for lunches, sorted gear, burned food scraps from the garbage bag, and did other general housework while waiting for the break we needed to proceed.

While we teetered at the stage of deciding whether to spend the night here or push on, there was a brief window in the gale. The old adage is true: "If you don't like the weather in B.C., wait five minutes." In this case we had waited five hours, but it does illustrate a point. We hastily launched with twenty knots of wind out of the southeast. With an all-or-nothing sprint we managed to pull out around Jeddah Point, thrash across

Halfmoon Bay in a beam sea and onto the beach at Redroofs Park.

By this time it was definitely the camp-searching hour and with a solid line of cottages along the shore, we had a challenge on our hands. I dug out my stash of quarters, found a pay phone, and spent some time calling local bed and breakfast establishments, hoping that one might perchance have water access. But no luck. Most were booked solid or were far too far away to trudge to with our boats. Jaquie stood on the sea wall watching our gear and a family loading a powerboat onto a trailer on the boat ramp. Demonstrating her outgoing manner yet again, she wandered over to chat, explaining our problem and asking for any suggestions on the local camp areas. This lovely family saw our dilemma and invited two complete strangers back to their home for a grassy camp on their lawn, just a few hundred yards along the shore!

We pulled up in front of their beach home, and they directed us to a quiet spot in the back yard, even offering us the use of a washroom in the unused guesthouse. After we settled a bit, we met the rest of the family who were still gathered for an annual summer vacation. We spent a wonderful evening with them, relating our adventures and finding we have friends in common at home in Vancouver.

Next morning we woke to the fragrance of freshly brewed coffee being served at our tent. Not often have we enjoyed such remarkable hospitality. *Wow, what a treat!* As we made our breakfast and packed we could sense their curiosity at our gear and supplies. One or the other of the family found a reason to wander past our packing area, asking about this and that, or exclaiming about the unlikelihood of all the clutter eventually fitting back into the boats. The ritual packing took a little longer than usual. We lingered for one last cup of coffee, a bit more conversation, and then turned to see a bay of mud before us, as the water was rapidly retreating.

Grandma, Grandpa, and a lovely granddaughter all pulled on their rubber boots, picked up a bag or two, and helped us ferry the boats and gear over the mud to the nearest water deep enough to float the kayaks. We were trying to launch on one of the lowest tides of the year. Eventually afloat, we waved good-bye, promising to keep in touch, and set off into a sou'westerly wind. The sea built up as we passed Merry Island and rounded Reception Point. We were headed for Sechelt, and the Trail Islands gave us small respite from the swells. We pulled into the beach for lunch and a rest. The leg from Halfmoon Bay to Selma Park was a short three and a half hours and nine miles, but still was a hard slog.

We were welcomed by our good friends Jean and Peter at Selma Park and spent a very pleasant evening with them. By this time we must have appeared like odd apparitions to folks who had known us only in civilized social circles. My hair had grown long, with wild curls hanging over my ears and in my eyes, my beard was varying shades of grey and red, and I'd grown leaner than I'd been in recent years. Our skin was weathered and salt-rimed, our clothing faded from the constant exposure. When we were ushered into our quarters and caught a full view of ourselves in the mirror, we looked with wonder at the two lean, ruddy faces peering back at us. It was no longer a puzzle why the folks we meet are curious about what we have seen and done over the previous weeks. Recounting the best bits of the trip and sharing a meal, we looked out over the sea that we love so well. Late in the evening we retired to a beautiful room with a comfortable bed, and slept like royalty.

August 17th

When we wandered up the stairs to the kitchen, Jean was cooking a big pot of oatmeal for us, and the steaming hot coffee smelled delicious. As we sat with Jean and Peter, we watched the flat sea ebbing and the wind rising. With two days to go on our journey, we bade our friends farewell and made our way slowly into the sou'wester towards Howe Sound. For two hours we slogged into breaking head seas until the conditions moderated as we rounded Gower Point into Howe Sound. We tied up the boats at a float in Gibsons Landing and found a telephone.

A glimmer of reality dawned as we talked to our welcoming committee at home. Our friends and families wouldn't be able to meet us on the 20th because it is a Monday – a workday. At first this seemed difficult for wanderers like us, but a heated discussion ensued over a burger and coffee. We could arrive at the beach in North Vancouver with no transportation home on the Monday, or we could press on and get home tomorrow, a Sunday. Although I was reluctant to commit to crossing Howe Sound without an extra day for weather insurance, there was no question in Jaquie's mind. She'd caught the scent of home. The late lunch fortified us for the crossing to Plumper Cove on Keats Island, which would be the last night of the trip.

Jaquie:

What a wonderful thing to put coins into a black box and be rewarded with the voices of my children and grandson! I must be slipping into some maudlin state of dotage – I want to smell their hair, hug them all, hold my tiny granddaughter in my arms, and feel her heart against mine. Rick argues we need to keep a day up our sleeves for poor weather and could spend an extra day on Keats or Bowen Islands, but I need to go home. Tomorrow. I long for my family. We call them back and make arrangements for the time and the beach.

Plumper Cove is busy with campers and picnickers, but we had no trouble finding a good tent site with a table and all the amenities of a marine park. A large family picnicing close by gave us a cooked crab and a parcel of new potatoes with garlic. After learning where we have been they must have imagined we had been suffering hard times and lean pickings. After the decadent and hefty portions at dinner, we savoured a cool beer and talked about home. We looked in vain for a member of the multitudes of raccoons that have inhabited the park in the past. Rumour has it that their numbers were recently decimated by rabies.

Sunday, August 19th

Despite a noisy night in the campground at Plumper Cove, we were up with the birds. The pack and carry went seamlessly and we were across to the top of Bowen Island and down to Snug Cove for lunch. From there we phoned our families to give them an ETA at Ambleside Beach in West Vancouver and started the last significant crossing. For a summer Sunday, ferry and other boat traffic in Howe Sound was reasonably quiet, and we made good time.

The traverse past Fisherman's Cove to Point Atkinson and the old lighthouse was pure delight in the late summer sunshine. We could easily have been on a half-day paddle out of West Vancouver. As we rounded Point Atkinson we were faced with the office towers of downtown Vancouver. We puttered along in culture shock, gazing at the waterfront mansions of West Vancouver. Here and there folks on patios under big umbrellas would wave at us, toasting with a cool glass of something-or-other. The burnt-sugar smell of barbecues and hamburger fat wafted across the water, mixed with a combination of diesel fumes and suntan oil. Powerboats rushed to and fro at a tremendous speed. Or was it just that we were so very slow? We seemed to be in a dream where we were going to wake up like Rip van Winkle and find that the world had changed.

I asked Jaquie, "Are you ready for this? Or should we keep on going to California?" She seemed to waver before replying, "If our families weren't waiting for us at Ambleside . ." Ah well, another trip, another time. Throughout our summer, moving south day after day, week after week, I'd visualized our homecoming. It would be a beautiful summer afternoon when we pulled up on yellow sand. Our families would be there. It's amazing how a vision can be reproduced in reality so faithfully.

After what seemed an age, there is the beach. We scouted

out a spot with the fewest bodies and gently 'shooshed' onto the sand. We scanned faces up and down the stretch of beach, searching for a familiar smile. We seemed to have arrived too early! But not to worry, we decided we'd have an ice cream and relax into the bustle of a vaguely familiar environment.

But then one... two friends... and then groups of family began to hurry over the sand! There were big hugs all round. Everyone was laughing and trying to cover a summer's news all at once. There were balloons and T-shirts freshly-printed with "We made it!" slogans, chocolate and flowers and happy voices chattering. We loaded all our gear and kayaks onto my truck and then all went off to a restaurant for a meal and the biggest, longest talk of all.

Jaquie:

I hold my granddaughter in my arms for what seems forever, burying my nose in her hair, joyfully inhaling the sweet baby smell of her, while my grandson asks questions and plays at my feet in the sand. He seems a bit confused by the whole situation, and probably wishes he could just have an ice cream cone and leave the adults to their nattering. I know he will sit quietly with me in the coming days, enjoying stories of whales and bears and wolves. My heart fills with peace, promise and an enormous sense of completion as I gaze from one pair of smiling eyes to the next, the warm conversation floating around me. Never will I wander without this joy in coming home.

Epilogue

Here on the North American 49th parallel we have conflict between snowmobilers, skiers, and snow shoers. We allocate specific areas for each activity. On the water, self-propelled or wind-propelled craft conflict with those powered by the 'infernal' combustion engine. Long negotiations take place to 'manage' the land and the sea. Kayakers view speeding pleasure craft as dangerous and polluting. Some powerboaters see kayakers as demented Luddites – a danger to everyone including themselves, and a burden on the Coast Guard. Kayakers coming ashore at dusk find they have to put to sea again because the beach is crammed with members of guided parties already encamped there. Everyone dreams of a beach cottage of their own, but one that has the rest of the shoreline undeveloped. There are just too many of us concentrated in one place.

The vast majority of people out 'recreating' in kayaks, powerboats, sail boats or onshore are reasonable, ordinary folks like us. En masse we have conflict, alienating the 'other side' while fighting for our piece of the action. We might be part of the problem instead of part of the solution.

There are good organizations in British Columbia dedicated to preserving these wild areas, such as the Georgia Strait Alliance, the Outdoor Recreation Council of B.C., and the Federation of Mountain Clubs. Dedicated people are making amazing progress at increasing public awareness of the need to work together to protect what we have. These organizations struggle along on volunteerism and minimum funding. I wonder if we will be boating on toxic pea soup before more of us realize we have to do something about pollution in the strait. Maybe a black line around an iceberg in the Southern Ocean is of no concern to a Northern Hemisphere boat owner with dirty fuel injectors, but the Orcas know. Anyone who spends time close to, or beneath the ocean knows. It's time. It's past time. The clock is ticking. We must do something now and we must do it cooperatively.

Jaquie:

As I work to edit this manuscript so many months after landing on that last beach, I have occasion to consider my concerns, joys and goals ruminated upon during the long hours of paddling.

My career has changed. I no longer work full time in an office, but spend my time working with my son and our bees, inspecting apiaries of other beekeepers to help them combat diseases, pests and parasites and enjoy the company of my Nova Scotia Duck Toller pup as we travel through the Fraser Valley.

Rick and I have traveled to Vietnam where he works to assist ethnic villagers develop sustainable community tourism, and I work with subsistence farmers to increase their honey production from their local native bees. We have rafted on the Paquare River in Costa Rica, kayaked in Belize and Halong Bay in Vietnam. Our lives are filled with challenge and fun, and the work we do is fulfilling.

We kayak, hike and ski or snowshoe with family and friends, and delight in sharing our outdoor playground with our grandchildren. How satisfying it is to see the wonder in their bright young faces as they spot tiny freshwater shrimp in a lake bottom, pick wild huckleberries, catch toads or examine spider webs covered in necklaces of dew.

When people ask us what we'll be doing when we retire

we wonder how to answer. It doesn't seem possible that retirement could be any better than this life we lead at present.

Acknowledgements:

Sincere thanks to all the good West Coast folks who contributed to our adventure. Specifically we would like to thank the following for their generosity....

Dorothy and Brian Vezina for sharing their hard seafaring experiences on the North Coast;

Peter McGee for showing us many routes and waterways in the complexity of the passages;

Jody Simmonds of the "La Niña" Expedition for sharing logistics and campsites with us;

All the folks in the Sea Kayak Association of British Columbia, who supplied parts of the mosaic that made up the plan;

The unknown lady at Klemtu who shared her snapper and canned salmon with us;

Penny Birnbaum who shared her solo adventures and precious campsites from the north and central coasts;

Cris Boyd and Larry McGregor who were there for us with support at the beginning and at the final landing;

Violet Neasloss at Klemtu for her generosity, stories, and explanations of the ancient art of cedar strip weaving;

The prawn fishermen in Skene Cove who provided us the raw material for honey-garlic prawns, the highlight of a very damp camp;

The generous people in Oona River who gave us cheese and eggs;

The crew of the "LSD" who made us hot tea and shared some supplies during a miserable southerly slog in Laredo Channel;

Mina and Leonard Werseen and their family who invited us to camp on their lawn and welcomed us into their home at Halfmoon Bay;

Jean and Peter Rice who provided a wonderful evening at their home in Sechelt – a shower, the luxury of clean sheets and a lovely meal;

Evan Loveless of Klemtu Tourism who made us very welcome;

Our children, Kristin, Sally, Scott, and Mark who supported us in every way throughout the journey. Grandchildren Sam and Kaitlyn who inspire us to share the outdoors we love;

Heidi Greco, our editor, – her encouragement and insight enabled us to tell our story;

Kelly Everaert, whose drawings enhance our pages;

J V G Smith, artist, photographer and friend – thanks for the Island poem so many years ago!

References:

The Birds of Canada – Godfrey, W. Earl

Common Birds of British Columbia – Sept, J. Duane

Tidepool and Reef – Harbo, Rick M.

Coastal Villages – Kennedy, Liv

www.laxkwalaams.ca

http://www.schoolnet.ca/autochtone/umista1/index-e.html

Technical Information

Challenges Anticipated:

Repetitive strain injury, traumatic injury, psychological depression, Cape Caution, cruise ship crossings, fog, storms, Slingsby Channel, tidal rapids (Whirlpool, Greene Point, Dent and Yaculta), equipment failure.

Statistics:

Planned length of journey	532 nm
Actual length of journey	602 nm
Planned duration	66 days
Actual Duration	65 days
Paddling days	56 days
Storm days/ rest days	9 days
Average speed	2 knots
Average paddling time per day	5 hrs
Average daily distance (based on whole trip)	9 nm
Average daily distance (based on paddling days)	11 nm
Longest day on the water	21 nm/13 hrs

Equipment List:

2 tree hooks and pulleys, 80 ft of 6mm prussic line for hauling food, haul bags;

Repair kit with fibreglass putty, tools, duct tape, epoxy, leather, nylon fabric, sailmaker's palm, waxed thread and needles and 40 feet of nylon cord for general use;

Personal Flotation Device with knife, flares, survival kit, carabiners, rope, sunglasses, VHF radio, spare battery pack, compass, whistle, binoculars, sunscreen, power bars and toque;

Fishing kit (hand reel, buzz bombs, hooks, licence, jigging lures, mesh bag, cord, fish bonker);

First aid kit;

Kayaks with paddles and spare paddlse, paddle leash, drip rings, Brittlestar self-rescue floats, bow and stern lines, deck lines, cameras, sunhats, tow line, parachute flare, bear spray, sponges, chart case, pumps, sprayskirts, water bottles, thermos and mid-wheels;

Tarp, tent, fly, lantern, 5 candles, pegs and poles in compression sack, and garbage bags;

26 litres of fresh water in 2 dromedaries and 1 reliance bottle, "Pristine" water purifier;

2 pots, MSR Whisperlite stove and repair kit, mugs, spoons, 3 litres of white gas, outback oven, pot scourer, pot lifter, corkscrew, fry pan, whisk, food, fire grill, 50 feet of aluminum foil, snacks, and drinks;

Shipmaster tide tables, detailed current tables of Dent and Yuculta, navigation instruments, 23 charts in a 30-litre drybag, journal, pens, pencils, eraser, wallet and $300 cash, cheque book, envelopes, stamps, keys, 30 large Ziplock bags for charts;

Broadcast radio receiver, books, backgammon game, washing gear, radio charger, 30 firelighter sticks, toilet paper;

Polartec 100 fleece pants, quick-dry long pants, 2 pairs of wool socks each, 2 polypropylene shirts each, dry fleece jackets, wet fleece jackets, fleece vests, quick-dry shorts, denim shorts and belt, spare toques, shortsleeved fleeces, 2 bandannas, waterproof jackets, Teva sandals, Farmer John wetsuits, cotton T-shirts, cotton sunshirts, shoes;

Synthetic sleeping bags rated to -7 degrees Celsius, with stuff sacks and drybags, Thermarest sleeping mattresses with drybags;

Pruning shears and hand chainsaw, Petzl headlamps, spare battery, 48 spare AA cells, spare camera battery.

Food List:

We adopted the 'pantry' system where meals are made from bulk staples, rather than the 'menu' system where all meals are pre-bagged. This has the advantage of less packaging, flexible choice of meals and easier packing in the boats. Our range of cooked food covered pizza, bread, brownies, cornbread, muffins, cookies, upside-down cake, chicken pot pie, iced cake and focaccia bread. The disadvantage of the pantry system is the time finding, sorting, preparing and cooking food. We took 200 pounds of food with us for the first month, then re-supplied along the way. Band stores were excellent, particularly Kitkatla, Klemtu and Bella Bella. Marina stores often did not have staples.

Our food list was as follows:

Fresh foods: potato, yam, carrot, cabbage, garlic, oranges, cheese, fish as we caught it;

Brown rice, pasta, flour, cornmeal, milk powder, oatmeal, margarine, Uncle Ben's flavoured rice, home-made granola;

Spices and condiments: Nutmeg, cinnamon, oregano, rosemary, curry, beef stock, chicken stock, dried coconut, cocoa, salt, pepper, olive oil, baking powder, baking soda, dried soups, coconut milk powder, yeast, oxtail soups, parmesan cheese, sugar, raisins, dates, nuts;

Dehydrated onions, corn, garlic, pasta sauce, tomato, potato, mushrooms, peas;

Four-litre bag of red wine, Grand Marnier;

Instant coffee, ground coffee, filters, hot chocolate, tea;

Honey, pancake mix, pancake syrup, trail mix;

Canned tuna, salmon, chicken, corned beef, baked beans, tomato paste, fruit, refried beans.

Basic Bread

Use the same recipe as for the pizza crust, but double it. I like to use other grains, a bit of granola, flax seed, or other stuff that looks and tastes good. I still use some flour to give it a bit of a softer texture if I use nuts and things. You can add your favourite herbs, or sun-dried tomato or a bit of zucchini or onion for a change.

Rise the dough for 23 to 30 minutes, punch it down (just make a fist and plough it down into the dough to release the big bubbles, then fold it a little bit — not too much or it will get tough — and rise it a second time for up to an hour. It should double in size if things are working right. You may have to use the stove or oven to warm it up a bit if it's a cold day. Bake it for about 45 minutes. Not quite as hot as for cornbread, though.

Hint: You can use a bread machine mix if you want the convenience.

Cornbread

1 cup flour
¼ cup sugar
4 tsp. baking powder
¾ cup salt
or olive oil

1 cup cornmeal
2 eggs
1 cup milk
¼ cup soft shortening

Combine the dry ingredients in your biggest bowl or pot, stir in the cornmeal. Whisk up the eggs in your mug or measuring cup. Use a fork if you didn't bring along a whisk. Add the milk and shortening or oil (I prefer oil, as it will mix in even on a cold, rainy day under the tarp) and stir it up to blend it, then add it to the dry ingredients and beat it in just until it's smooth. Pour it into a greased pan or non-stick out door oven pan, and bake it in a fairly hot oven (425 degrees Celsius) or just as hot as you can get it without it beginning to burn. Check it frequently and adjust the heat of your stove as needed. Shouldn't take much more than 25 to 30 minutes unless there is a stiff wind.

If it turns out, it's guaranteed to amaze at a marina potluck.

Upside Down Cake

Basic Cake

1¼ cups flour
½ tsp salt
2 eggs (or 2 tbsp powdered eggs)
2/3 cup br sugar (or honey and reduce the water a bit)
1 tsp vanilla
1½ tsp baking powder
1/3 cup oil
½ cup water or milk

First mix up the flour, salt and baking powder, then mix up the rest of the ingredients in a separate pot or bowl. Then combine everything and stir it up until its fairly smooth.

In the baking pan, heat some butter or oil and add honey or brown sugar, and mix it up until it is all melted and blended. Then put in some fruit such as canned peaches, apricots, pineapple or mandarin orange segments. Fresh fruit is best, but how long can you keep it in a kayak? Next, pour in the batter, bake it for about 20 minutes and take the lid off the oven or pan for the last few minutes. You can serve it right out of the pan, or invert it onto a plate for maximum crowd appeal.

Other Cakes

Use the basic cake recipe but reduce the flour by ¼ cup and add ¼ cup cocoa powder for a chocolate cake. I like to throw in some nuts if I have them.

Other flavours can be created by eliminating the vanilla and adding your favourite such as lemon juice, remembering to reduce the water by the amount of juice you're adding so the cake doesn't get too goopy.

Pizza — basic crust

2/3 cup warm water	1 pkg. active dry yeast
1 tsp sugar	2 tbsp oil
2 cups flour (approx.)	½ tsp salt

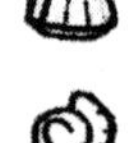

Blend all the ingredients in a pot or a bowl (if you brought one) then mix in warm not hot, water. Once blended, knead it for about 5 minutes. If it's too sticky, add more flour. Then stretch it out into your pizza pan, or out back oven pan. Cover it up and put a fleece jacket over it if it's a cold, windy day. Or use the oven to rise it. Yeast likes to be warm to grow. Let it rise for 5 to 15 minutes.

Toppings

Use your imagination. Lots of cheeses do well. We really like parmesan for all kinds of meals, so it usually goes on the pizza along with whatever else we have – cheddar, mozza, romano. Take one of those little tubes of tomato paste and mix it up with some garlic, Italian spices, chilis, olive oil or whatever you fancy. A 10 inch pizza only needs about 3 or 4 tbsp. of sauce. Whisk it up, and spread it on the dough, then pop on your favourite stuff like mushrooms, sun-dried tomatoes, pepperoni or whatever you have along that tastes good. You can soften dehydrated veg. in some warm water while you make the dough. If you overload on the goodies, it won't cook as well, so make more than one pizza. On goes the cheese, pop it into your oven and it should take about 20 or 25 minutes. If you use the lid on your oven, try setting the lid ajar to crisp things up a bit. Or take off the lid and just use your convection dome. Just remember to clean it up after you've finished so your dessert won't taste like pizza.

Tamale Pie

If you have some onions and crushed chilis, maybe some dehy mushrooms, sautée the fresh veg or soak the dyhy veggies. Set them aside for a minute. Mix up a half batch of cornbread. Use black bean flakes or other dehydrated beans, and make up enough for 2 cups cooked beans using cold water, and let it sit until all the water is soaked up. Spoon it over the batter in the pan and bake it for about 20 to 25 minutes. Mix up the veggies and the beans and put it on top of the cornbread. I like some cheese or chopped wild onion, or some celery or cilantro or chopped sun-dried tomatoes in it too, just for variety. Especially on those cold evenings when you can feel the damp soaking into your bones, your enthusiasm is flagging and your body needs some caloric assistance.

Chart List:

(FROM NORTH TO SOUTH)

(1). Ketchikan U.S. 17434
(2) Portland Canal 3960
(3) Hudson Bay passage 3954
(4) Prince Rupert 3957
(5) Bonilla Island 3927
(6) Hecate Strait 3902
(7) Otter Passage to Bonilla Is.3741
(8) Otter Passage to McKay Reach 3742
(9) Camano Sound 3742
(10) Milbanke Sound 3728
(11) Idol Point to Ocean Falls 3720
(12) Namu Harbour to Dryad Point 3785
(13) Queen Charlotte Strait (Western)
(14) Queen Charlotte Sound 3744
(15) Quatsino Sound to Queen Charlotte Strait 3605
(16) Queen Charlotte Strait (Central) 3584
(17) Queen Charlotte Strait (Eastern) 3547
(18) Broughton Strait 3546
(19) Johnstone Strait, Port Neville to Robson Bight 3545
(20) Johnstone Strait, Race Passage & Current Passage 3544
(21) Cordero Channel 3543
(22) Canadian Hydrographic Current sharts on Yaculta Rapids
(23) Toba inlet 3541
(24) Strait of Georgia (Northern) 3513
(25) Strait of Georgia (Central) 3512

ISBN 141208091-6

9 781412 080910